PSYCHOLOGY RESEARCH PROGRESS

BORN BAD?

CRITIQUES OF PSYCHOPATHY

PSYCHOLOGY RESEARCH PROGRESS

Additional books in this series can be found on Nova's website under the Series tab.

Additional e-books in this series can be found on Nova's website under the e-book tab.

PSYCHIATRY - THEORY, APPLICATIONS AND TREATMENTS

Additional books in this series can be found on Nova's website under the Series tab.

Additional e-books in this series can be found on Nova's website under the e-book tab.

PSYCHOLOGY RESEARCH PROGRESS

BORN BAD?

CRITIQUES OF PSYCHOPATHY

JAMES HORLEY
EDITOR

NOVINKA

New York

Library of Congress Cataloging-in-Publication Data

Born bad? : critiques of psychopathy / [edited by] James Horley (University of Alberta, Camrose, Alberta, Canada).
pages cm
Includes bibliographical references and index.
ISBN 978-1-62618-082-6 (soft cover)
1. Antisocial personality disorders. 2. Psychopaths. 3. Psychopaths--Legal status, laws, etc. I. Horley, James, 1954-
RC555.B67 2013
616.85'82--dc23

2013004720

Published by Nova Science Publishers, Inc. † New York

CONTENTS

PREFACE

Psychopathy is a construct encountered with increased frequency especially for those professionals who work in forensic mental health. Psychopathy, unfortunately, is a troublesome term to use in any context. Various problems and issues plague psychopathy; the term itself is unclear, as is its many variations, and even the typical understanding of the history of the construct is open to dispute. The prescribed response of mental health professionals to the treatment of psychopathy is confused and confusing. In short, the problems associated with psychopathy are broad and serious.

This volume arises from the need to provide serious examinations of psychopathy's contentious issues. All three contributors to this book have worked in various prisons and forensic settings. By my reckoning, we have more than 60 years of clinical and research experience in total. During our years working with criminal offenders or those individuals found not criminally responsible for their acts, we have come across many individuals, probably a majority, who have been branded as psychopaths, sociopaths, antisocial personality disordered, or any number of other related diagnoses. The problem with all such labels is that they are imprecise and carry serious legal and treatment connotations. They also involve many unresolved issues of greater or lesser significance, and it is the more serious of these issues that we will address in this book. These issues range from historical concerns, such as the origins of the construct, to pragmatic ones, such as the efficacy of psychopathy treatments. Even some broad issues of concern beyond the field of forensic mental health, such as the impact of the label psychopathy, are considered. It is intended to stimulate thought and to provide solutions to the problems that plague psychopathy and any professional who would employ it.

A couple of notes about the book are necessary at the beginning. At times, the term psychopathy will be used to include all similar constructs such as sociopathy and antisocial personality disorder. There are too many related notions to list all of them and it is just too clumsy to repeat "psychopathy and all its variants". We would also note that while we may, at times, call an individual a psychopath, there are inverted commas implied on all of these uses. Again, it is just too clumsy to do this each time. We would have each reader consider, however, whether each or any use of the label is warranted or justified as an important psychological predicate.

There are many people who were key in bringing this book project to fruition. No doubt the project would not have begun if not for the suggestion of Nadya Columbus of Nova Science. Also at Nova, Christine Sheehan has kept the project on track since it began. Dr. Jan Clarke of Algoma University deserves thanks for her careful reading and helpful suggestions of portions of this work. We would also like to thank all of our forensic colleagues and clients, past and present, who have contributed to our insights on this topic. They are too numerous to mention here.

Jim Horley, Ph.D., Editor,
University of Alberta,
Camrose, Alberta, Canada

In: Born Bad? Critiques of Psychopathy
Editor: James Horley
ISBN: 978-1-62618-082-6

Chapter 1

AN OVERVIEW OF SOME ISSUES IN THE STUDY OF PSYCHOPATHY

James Horley*
University of Alberta, Camrose, Alberta, Canada

INTRODUCTION

The term "psychopath" is very common in contemporary parlance. Many forensic psychologists and psychiatrists employ it on a daily basis, and many modern crime writers and Hollywood screen writers have embraced the notion. Ignoring the frequent use of "psycho" to refer to psychopathy, psychosis, or at times any unspecified psychological problem, the expectation of many of us is that psychopathy is a well understood psychiatric illness/condition/disorder with well known etiology, symptoms and prognosis. Unfortunately for both specialist and non-specialist alike, this is not the case. Since its inception, psychopathy has proven to be a problematic notion fraught with looseness in meaning and troublesome practical implications (e. g., use and outcomes in criminal courts). Indeed, its use has been so confusing and controversial that there are now a set of terms—such as antisocial personality disorder, psychopathic personality, sociopathy—that share much of the same intent as psychopathy but with somewhat different shades of meaning.

* Email: jhorley@ualberta.ca

A very critical examination of psychopathy appears necessary and the present volume will attempt such an examination. The concerns and critiques of the authors are very select—all are forensic psychologists with a research background who deliver clinical services to criminal offenders in a variety of forensic settings—but it is hoped and expected that many of our problems with psychopathy are also relevant to psychiatry and other mental health professions, to say nothing of the public who should be concerned about psychodiagnostic activities. The topics addressed here will range from historical to theoretical concerns and include more practical considerations relevant to treatment and assessment issues. They will not be exhaustive, and we leave further critiques to our colleagues and writers in forensic mental health and beyond.

Prior to dealing with our specific concerns, an introduction to the construct of psychopathy and its variants seems useful. Much has been said about psychopathy, and it not necessary here to cover all this territory. Interested readers will be provided with references at the end of each chapter that will provide much more information if desired.

Definitions of Psychopathy and Related Terms

There do not appear to be many concise definitions of psychopathy although there are many descriptions of the condition or characteristic expressions of the disorder; unfortunately, not all commentators are in agreement concerning the essential characteristics of a psychopath. Many of the descriptions have been provided by two main writers, Hervey Cleckley (1941, 1976) and Robert Hare (1970, 1993).

Cleckley (1941), though he preferred the term psychopathy, was one of the first clinical researchers to describe in detail the condition called psychopathic personality. For Cleckley, the psychopath was as an antisocial or at least asocial loner, someone completely self-preoccupied and totally unconcerned about the harm that they may inflict on others in the pursuit of their own interests, although Cleckley did not believe that they had an overall or coherent life plan. Psychopaths-- and while Cleckley (1941) did consider some women as psychopathic the vast majority were men-- possessed superficial charm in order to manipulate others but generally lacked any real social intelligence or ability to learn from their mistakes at all. Psychopaths lie constantly to those around them in order to manipulate or manage impressions; indeed, Cleckley went so far as to state that they lack the ability to perceive the difference between truth and falsehood. They lack any sense of responsibility and sense of guilt, lacking an ability to accept any blame for their own actions. In short, psychopaths are manipulative, dissembling, self-absorbed and possibly dangerous individuals, perhaps interesting to be around but only briefly. Cleckley's number of psychopathic characteristics did change over time (compare Cleckley, 1959, 1975) but the core of his description remained constant. Cleckley was also consistent insofar as he did not equate psychopathic personality and criminality except to suggest that crime, and subsequent punishment for that matter, meant nothing to a psychopath.

Although he tended to follow the lead of Cleckley, Hare (1970, 1993) developed an understanding of psychopathy more complex than Cleckley's view of the construct. Hare proposed two separate factors, an affective or interpersonal factor made up of numerous characteristics (e.g., glibness, shallow affect, lack of empathy) and a social deviance factor (e.g., impulsivity, criminal versatility, parasitic lifestyle). As well, each of the two factors has two facets. Hare (1993) emphasized that, like Cleckley, while psychopaths may be incarcerated for some of their criminal activities, psychopathy is not synonymous with criminality. Psychopaths, for Hare, are glib, slick, fast-talking, thrill-seeking, irresponsible, and reckless individuals who are unconcerned about the pain or inconvenience that they cause for others—they are utterly self-obsessed and only pursue personal ends. This broader view of psychopathy has been emphasized by Hare and colleagues (e.g., Babiak and Hare, 2006).

Other writers have a somewhat different take on psychopathy. Wilson and Herrnstein (1985), for example, have described psychopathy as "the prime criminogenic personality trait" (p. 198). This flies in the face of most other views of psychopathy by reducing it to a single characteristic as opposed to a syndrome or collection of traits. From their rather unique and extreme position, Wilson and Herrnstein only recognize the overlap between psychopathy and criminality and not the possibilities that non-criminals may also qualify as psychopaths.

Sociopathy is a relatively recent notion relative to psychopathy yet the two are related. Sociopathy tends to emphasize specific abnormal reactions to abnormal social conditions rather than antisocial traits. Antisocial responses or behaviors of some individuals are the emphasis of sociopathy, especially those who respond in a habitually antisocial manner, essential sociopaths (Partridge, 1930), to conditions that are not acceptable or conducive to particular individuals.

The term 'psychopathic personality', although seen by some clinicians as synonymous with psychopathy (e. g., Dolan, 2004), seems to have a slightly different meaning, and one that is problematic (Lewis, 1973). Developed initially to describe an intellectual or psychological weakness, it soon became attached to antisocial and criminal behavior (Gurvitz, 1951), especially through the work of Kraepelin (1907). Psychopathic personality came to refer in general to a set of traits or characteristics including egocentrism, arrogance, irresponsibility, and a lack of concern for the welfare of others as individuals with psychopathic traits engage in manipulation, deception, and dishonesty. The term is now more common in Europe than in North America, where psychopathy is much more common, along with the psychiatric disorder antisocial personality disorder.

The American Psychiatric Association has expanded the acceptance of the notion of psychopathic personality although it has not necessarily clarified our understanding of psychopathy. The first version of the *Diagnostic and Statistical Manual of Mental Disorders (DSM*; APA, 1952) included sociopathic personality disturbance under the category of personality disorder, which was described as "developmental defects or pathological trends in personality structure… manifested by a lifelong pattern of action or behavior, rather than by mental or emotional symptoms" (p. 34). Thus, while the Association appeared to be adopting the notion of sociopathy, the former idea of psychopathic personality seemed at the core of the category. Adding to the confusion were the sub-types of sociopathy, including "antisocial reaction" and "sexual deviation", that were in general described as a lack "of conformity with the prevailing cultural milieu" (p. 38). Subsequent editions of the *DSM* eliminated the term 'sociopathy', settling instead on antisocial personality disorder in the most recent version of the manual (APA, 2000). While antisocial personality disorder may eliminate some internal inconsistency by pointing to the defective traits of individuals that produce antisocial behavior, it is distinctive from psychopathy and even sociopathy insofar as its focus is behavior especially criminal behavior. While the differences may appear small, they exist nonetheless, and some efforts (e.g., Hare, Hart, and Harpur, 1991) have been made to resolve some of the differences among the various terms that appear similar.

Antisocial personality disorder, at least according to the American Psychiatric Association, refers to repeated violation of others' rights, since 15 years of age, and including at least three or more of failure to conform to social norms, deceitfulness, impulsivity, irritability-aggression, reckless disregard for safety, irresponsibility, and a lack of remorse. Additionally, the individual must be at least 15 years old and evidence of a conduct disorder. A conduct disorder is an emotional and behavioral disorder of childhood and adolescence where individuals act out aggressively and angrily towards people, animals, and objects, and it is characterized by irritability and low self-esteem (APA, 2000).

The World Health Organisation's *International Statistical Classification of Diseases and Related Health Problems - 10th Revision (ICD-10)* is a detailed compendium of physical and psychological disorders (WHO, 2004). Like the *DSM*, the *ICD* has undergone various changes in terminology relevant to mental health. Originally the term 'sociopathic personality' appeared. *ICD-10* now employs a diagnosis nearly identical to antisocial personality disorder, dissocial personality disorder, in its chapter on mental and behavioral disorders. Similar to antisocial personality disorder, the dissocial disorder involves a number of criteria indicative of a lack of regard for other individuals. These diagnostic criteria include a lack of concern for others' feelings, a low frustration tolerance with likelihood to employ aggression or violence, a tendency to blame others, and a lack of capacity to experience guilt. Clearly, like antisocial personality disorder, dissocial personality disorder emphasizes antisocial behavior related to problems with the law and, as such, differs somewhat from the notion of psychopathy. In terms of differences, dissocial subsumes antisocial and other personality disorders (e.g., asocial) in the *ICD-10* listing, and it seems to focus more on affective deficits than actual antisocial behavior (for a detailed discussion, see Ogloff, 2006).

It would probably be fair to conclude that confusion is the result of the aforementioned terminology, to say nothing of the dozens of additional terms related to these constructs (see Werlinder, 1978), rather than anything approaching clarification. The proliferation of psychopathy-related terms is perhaps, first-and-foremost, a reflection of the disagreements among those specialists in psychiatry and psychology who would employ such constructs, although the complexity of the issues pertaining to psychopathy may lead to some of the disagreements over terminology and definitions.

Born Bad, Made Bad, Both, or Neither?

There have been dozens of attempts to explain psychopathy. Levenson (1992) proposed that the 'traditional' explanations of psychopathy can be slotted into one of three categories: biological, developmental, and sociological. In a sense, this perspective conforms to the more medical understanding of biogenesis, psychogenesis, and sociogenesis, a perspective that emphasizes causal factors. If such a scheme is considered, biological or biosocial accounts are by far the most numerous and undoubtedly the most popular among researchers and clinicians interested in the nature of the psychopath.

Although not the first to suggest psychopathic biogenesis, Cleckley (1941) believed that psychopathy was innate and that psychopaths were born bad. He posited that some physiological mechanism could explain the psychopath's behavior, although he was not sure about the specific nature of such a biological problem. Lykken provided perhaps the earliest, detailed hypothesis about the cause of psychopathy (see Lykken, 2003). According to Lykken, a neural inhibitory system that regulates behavior can be defective in that fear in anticipation of punishment is missing and, as a consequence, there is a behavioral restraint deficit. Psychopaths, who are said to be fearless or lack anxiety in the face of danger, and data from various research supports, suffer from "inherent peculiarities of temperament" (Lykken, 2003, p. 7). Hare (1970), too, provided a rather specific, neurological explanation of psychopathy. Hare tested a group of adult male psychopaths using an electro-encephalogram and he found that they produced an odd pattern of brain waves much like the patterns displayed by children. Hare hypothesized that this child-like pattern accounted for the egocentric and fearless behavior seen in adult psychopaths and it also resulted in the improvement of behavior in many psychopaths during mid-life (see next section below). His "maturational lag hypothesis" was an innovative attempt to explain psychopathy. It lacks, unfortunately, much empirical support.

Development theories of psychopathy (e.g., Kegan, 1986) tend to emphasize familial or social environmental causal factors. During childhood and adolescence, according to this approach, some individuals experience emotional deprivation, lack of bonding, and/or social ostracism that prohibits their identification or concern with others' well-being (see McCord and McCord, 1964; Robins, 1966). In effect they are unable to acquire appropriate social values. The empirical support for such theories is lacking due, in large part, to the lack of longitudinal research on psychopathy (Lynam and Gudonis, 2005).

Sociological accounts of psychopathy have considered broader social environmental factors that may impact development. Gough (1948), for example, argued for a view of the psychopath as deficient in role-playing. From Gough's perspective, psychopaths are unable to adopt the role of the other in a significant way and hence are unable to understand and to relate meaningfully to social actors. According to Gough, this helps to explain psychopaths' social and legal conflicts as well as their limited emotional experiences. Unfortunately, he ignored the charm and social skills, however superficial, that such individuals use as a means of duping and using others. Robins (1966), too, relied on a sociological perspective to study 100s of high-risk children in the United States. After considering many demographic and psychiatric variables possibly related to sociopathy, Robins showed that there were a number of childhood factors (e.g., parental alcoholism, parental display of sociopathic characteristics) that determined subsequent sociopathic behavior in target children although, rather strangely, Robins emphasized biological aspects of her findings.

Another set of theories about psychopathy, generally more recent, include what can be seen as social psychological explanations. Levenson (1992), for example, wrote that psychopathy is not disease but a coherent philosophy of life that entailed at its center self-involvement and the trivialization of others. Levenson argued that, following a consideration of both biological and social explanations of psychopathy, the only reasonable explanation of psychopathy was that it involves learning not to experience social anxiety in situations that most people would find highly fearful. Some individuals as a result of their particular social experiences learn to overcome social anxiety and become social risk-takers, with a set of rewards for the successful that would encourage further risk-taking and even lower anxiety. Thus, for Levenson, psychopathy is not a disorder but an effect of learning circumstances. "Institutionalized psychopathy" (Levenson, 1992, p. 66) is a term to designate the distribution of destructive yet successful social acts across a wide range of activities within the context of a corporate culture. Whether business, politics, or the military, there are no doubt corporations that encourage behaviors that injure or kill others in the pursuit of the corporate agenda, and where success within the structure of the corporation demands acceptance of the values that encourage such values as might is right and those beyond the corporation do not matter. Through this psychosocial account of psychopathy, Levenson viewed psychopathy not just as a life philosophy or form of consciousness but as a conscious moral stance. He suggested rather ominously that this stance is becoming more acceptable in contemporary Western corporate life in particular and in the developed Western world generally.

It almost goes without saying that there is no widely accepted understanding of the origins of psychopathy. As mentioned, biogenetic accounts are most popular despite little consistent, replicated evidence to support any biological, neural, or innate explanation of psychopathy.

Undoubtedly such research will proceed but some of us who work with supposed psychopaths on a daily basis in forensic settings are not very optimistic about positive outcomes. Our pessimism is based, in part, on the inconsistent use of the various constructs, such as those described in the previous section as well as others. Even if definitions were to be clarified and terms used more consistently, there are many other impediments to finding evidence to support one explanation over others, and some of these issues will be addressed in this volume. It will be suggested that no explanation is sufficient here because there is nothing, at least nothing of a distinct innate nature, to explain.

PSYCHOPATHIC BURNOUT

One rather interesting and fairly consistent finding with respect to psychopathy and related notions is that they are not uniform throughout the life-span. This phenomenon has been referred to as 'psychopathic burnout' although the term has also included a number of other adjectives. Again, it no doubt reflects the rejection of psychopathy or any number of variants of the term.

Psychopathic burnout has been reported by a number of different researchers, especially Hare (Hare, 1970; Hare, McPherson, and Forth, 1988), and it refers to the tendency of antisocial and criminal behavior to decrease in mid-life among psychopaths. Hare, McPherson, and Forth (1988), for example, discovered that for male criminals over the age of 16 crime rates remained constant unless they were found to be psychopathic; if described as psychopaths, criminal activity remained high until around age 40 at which time it declined dramatically. It is worthwhile noting that they and others have found that a subset of the offenders diagnosed as psychopaths continue to offend beyond 40, and the key seems to be violence insofar as violent offenders continue to re-offend even into later life (Harris, Rice, and Cormier, 1991).

In a study of burnout in a sample diagnosed as antisocial personality disorder, Aboleda-Florez and Holley (1991) discovered similar results to the psychopathy findings but with some interesting differences. They found a decline in criminal activity among their male participants, although not all ceased antisocial behavior, but the age of decline was closer to 30 than 40. This age may well reflect the difference in diagnosis, and it may serve as a warning that all constructs related to psychopathy should not be regarded as synonymous.

The explanations for this burnout phenomenon have been relatively few and far between. Hare (1970) has offered his maturational lag hypothesis to account for burnout—the maturation of the neural structure of psychopaths is delayed until roughly age 40, at which time the brain becomes more like a regular adult brain and antisocial activity declines. Unfortunately, there appears to be very little evidence to support this hypothesis. A more straightforward explanation may involve a simple mechanism, insight. After spending 20 or 30 years using and abusing people, and likely finding that your efforts only produced enemies and prison sentences, in other words failure, is it not likely that a reasonably clever person would simply give up old patterns of behavior and old ways of thinking? While this may be the most parsimonious account of psychopathic burnout, it may not be the most compelling because of our own assumptions about the nature of anyone called a psychopath. My concern is that we, specialist and non-specialist alike, have come to individuals labeled psychopath, in general, as congenitally defective. Certainly we do not seem to credit them with the will or the agency to operate on their own in any way that is 'out of character' (e. g., pro-social, helpful). Perhaps this is a reasonable response to individually and collectively being taken advantage of repeatedly by someone or various persons, thus assuming that 'once a bastard, always a bastard'. Whatever the case, if we extend agency to all others just as we reserve it for ourselves, we might be able to see so-called 'psychopaths' and psychopathic burnout in a new light.

Summary and Conclusion

Everyone, either specialist or member of the general public, who is concerned about psychopathy is concerned with individuals who are considered dangerous to one degree or another. Psychopaths are regarded as self-preoccupied, irresponsible, dishonest, deceptive, manipulative thrill-seekers who have no regard for others' welfare, simply their own short-term interests. Although not necessarily involved in criminality, psychopaths are not deterred by criminal sanctions or any form of punishment. Psychopathy appears to be a very serious disorder yet it presents many baffling problems. Unfortunately, despite significant clinical and research attention especially over the past 20 years, the construct of psychopathy presents many unresolved issues and significant difficulties.

One obvious problem in this area concerns the proliferation of constructs and the differences, albeit sometimes slight, among all the various terms. The many related terms, some researchers (e. g., Werlinder, 1978) have pointed to as many as 150 distinct terms that have been used over the years, may reflect the complexity of psychopathy, but they may also reflect confusion about this controversial notion. There is no single definition or understanding of psychopathy and even terms that appear similar, like the contemporary construct of psychopathy and antisocial personality disorder, contain apparently minor yet important differences.

Another problem, which is no doubt related to the conceptual issue, is the lack of a comprehensive and acceptable explanation of the origin of psychopathy. While many specialists have proposed a variety of theories to account for psychopathy, there is a general acceptance that the disorder involves at least some unknown and perhaps very significant genetic or innate component. This problem of an unknown causation extends to the rather interesting burnout phenomenon, whereby some but by no means all psychopaths seem to leave their familiar and unsettling behavior behind around the age of 35 or 40 years. To call for more research would be trite, and it would not necessarily solve all the problems associated with the so-called psychopath. Further issues and problems, some rather broad and others much more specific, will be examined in detail in the following pages.

REFERENCES

American Psychiatric Association. (2000). *Diagnostic and statistical manual of mental disorders—Text revision (4th Edition)*. Washington: Author.

American Psychiatric Association. (1952). *Diagnostic and statistical manual of mental disorders*. Washington: Author.

Arboleda-Florez, J., and Holley, H. L. (1991). Antisocial burnout: An exploratory study. *Bulletin of the American Academy of Psychiatry and the Law*, 19, 173-183.

Cleckley, H. (1975). *The mask of sanity: An attempt to clarify some issues about the so-called psychopathic personality (5th Edition)*. St. Louis: Mosby.

Cleckley, H. (1959). Psychopathic states. In S. Arieti (Ed), *American handbook of psychiatry (Volume 1; pp.* 567-588). New York: Basic Books.

Cleckley, H. (1941). *The mask of sanity: An attempt to clarify some issues about the so-called psychopathic personality*. St. Louis: Mosby.

Dolan, M. (2004). Psychopathic personality in young people. *Advances in Psychiatric Treatment, 10,* 466-473.

Gough, H. G. (1948). A sociological theory of psychopathy. *American Journal of Sociology, 53,* 359-366.

Gurvitz, M. (1951). Developments in the concept of psychopathic personality (1900- 1950). *British Journal of Delinquency, 2,* 88-102.

Hare R. D. (1993). *Without conscience: The disturbing world of the psychopaths among us*. New York: Guilford.

Hare R. D. (1970). *Psychopathy: Theory and research*. New York: John Wiley and Sons.

Hare R. D., Forth, A. E., and Strachan, K. (1992). Psychopathy and crime across the life span. In R. D. Peters, R. J. McMahon, and V. L. Quinsey (Eds.), *Aggression and violence throughout the lifespan (pp. 285-300).* Newbury Park: Sage.

Hare R. D., Hart, S. D., and Harpur, T. J. (1991). Psychopathy and the DSM-IV criteria for antisocial personality disorder. *Journal of Abnormal Psychology, 100*, 391-398.

Hare, R. D., McPherson, L. M., and Forth, A. E. (1988). Male psychopaths and their criminal careers. *Journal of Consulting and Clinical Psychology, 56*, 710-714.

Harris, G. T., Rice, M. E., and Cormier, C. A. (1991). Psychopathy and violent recidivism. *Law and Human Behavior*, 15, 625-637.

Kegan, R. G. (1986). The child behind the mask. In W. Reid, G. Dorr, J. Walker, and J. Bonner (Eds.), *Unmasking the psychopath: Antisocial personality and related syndromes (pp. 45-77)*. New York: Norton.

Kraepelin, E. (1907). *Clinical psychiatry: A text-book for students and physicians*. New York: Macmillan Company.

Levenson, M. R. (1992). Rethinking psychopathy. *Theory and Psychology, 2,* 51-71.

Lewis, A. (1973). Psychopathic personality: A most elusive category. *Psychological Medicine, 4,* 133-140.

Lykken, D. T. (2003). Psychopathic personality: The scope of the problem. In C. J. Patrick (Ed.), *Handbook of psychopathy (pp.* 3-13). New York: Guilford.

Lynam, D. R., and Gudonis, L. (2005). The development of psychopathy. *Annual Review of Clinical Psychology, 1,* 381-407.

McCord, W, and McCord, J. (1964). *The psychopath: An essay on the criminal mind*. New York: Van Nostrand.

Ogloff, J. R.P. (2006). Psychopathy/antisocial personality disorder conundrum. *Australian and New Zealand Journal of Psychiatry, 40*, 519-528.

Partridge, G. E. (1930). Current conceptions of psychopathic personality. *American Journal of Psychiatry, 87*, 53-99.

Robins, L. N. (1966). *Deviant children grow up: A sociological and psychiatric study of sociopathic personality*. Baltimore: Williams and Wilkins.

Werlinder H. (1978). *Psychopathy: A history of the concepts*. Stockholm: Almquist and Wiksell.

Wilson, J. Q., and Herrnstein, R. J. (1985). *Crime and human nature*. New York: Simon and Shuster.

World Health Organization (2004). *International Statistical Classification of Diseases and Related Health Problems—10th Revision* (2nd Edition). Geneva: World Health Organization.

In: Born Bad? Critiques of Psychopathy
Editor: James Horley
ISBN: 978-1-62618-082-6

Chapter 2

A Brief History of Psychopathy

James Horley*
University of Alberta, Camrose, Alberta, Canada

Introduction

However popular psychopathy may be now in forensic mental health circles, this certainly was not always the case. Since psychopathy its variants first appeared there have been sharp divisions about the nature and importance of such a notion, even whether such a condition existed. A historical examination appears to be necessary in order to address issues of historical accuracy as well as to throw more light on specific meanings or connotations of the term, or more accurately terms, in the present.

As Temkin (1946) noted wisely, "Where history is lacking, mythology takes its place and those who disdain history are among the foremost victims of mythology" (p. 10). Berrios (1999), similarly, has pointed out that legend replaces actual history when writers accept well-repeated stories as fact. Whether it is called mythology or legend, the result of misinterpretation or reliance on faith that the stories told by prior authors are accurate, the history of the concept of psychopathy is littered with odd and misleading statements about the roots and the development of the notion. The origins and emergence of the current construct called psychopathy is obscured by false paths and connections, and misconnection impacts not only historical accuracy but the

* Email: jhorley@ualberta.ca

present connotations of the construct. Efforts to trace the history of the concept (e.g., Werlinder, 1978), therefore, are important studies.

Making sense of the story of psychopathy is complicated by the myriad of terms related to psychopathy. Werlinder (1978) lists several dozen different terms, and he noted that his list is not complete. There is no way that I will attempt to trace the origins of dozens of similar ideas here, nor would any reader likely desire it, so I will restrict attention to the main or common terms such as psychopathy, sociopathy, psychopathic personality, and antisocial personality disorder. Several additional ones might also be mentioned but only in passing.

The task of tracing the history of any construct, let alone a set of similar ones, is not a simple one because of the various languages, cultures, and disciplinary orientations of the notion, or seemingly similar notions. Indeed, the apparent timeframe of 200 years or more means that language, culture, and discipline change in spite of assumptions of constancy. The effort to unravel the historic confusion surrounding psychopathy and related terms is complicated by the existence of a number of related terms, some of which are used interchangeably with psychopathy but none of the terms seem truly synonymous. Certainly the meanings of any of the terms are far from clear. Despite these obstacles and despite my own limitations (i.e., predominant English speaker, alive in the 21st century, trained in psychology), it is my intent in this chapter to address through a historical examination some of the problems and confusions surrounding psychopathy, sociopathy, psychopathic personality, and similar terms.

Pinel, Rush, and the Early 19TH Century

Psychopathy has been traced by a variety of writers (e.g., Arrigo and Shipley, 2001; Gurvitz, 1951; Mason, 2006; Millon, Simonsen, and Birket-Smith, 1998; Waughs, 1941) to early 19th century work in mainstream psychopathology and psychiatric nosology. Even the roots of sociopathy have been seen placed in the middle of the 1800s (Barocas, 1970). The claim that seems to be made, often only between the lines, is that psychopathy has a long and noble history in modern psychiatry and psychology. Unfortunately, this does not appear to be the case. Even if true, one could question why, if this is such a serious and obvious condition, was it not recognised and described in some form before the 19th century, silly references to murder and psychopathy noted in the Biblical story of Cain and Abel aside. Psychopathy does not appear traceable to any period prior to the mid-20th century at least not in any substantial and recognisable form.

Most of the early attention concerned with the roots of psychopathy has been focussed on the famous French psychiatrist, Phillippe Pinel. As medical director of two French insane asylums, or early psychiatric facilities, Pinel is credited with being one of the first psychiatrists to introduce a more humane approach to psychiatric treatment, foregoing the chains used to restrain 'patients', really nothing more than inmates, and the whips employed to control and to 'treat' them. In his writings on psychiatric illnesses, Pinel (1801/1806) used the French term "manie sans delire" to refer to mania without delusion, or psychological disturbance without thought-disorder. It is this idea of mania without delusion or delirium that is claimed as the beginning of our modern notion of psychopathy. Unfortunately, as Whitlock (1982) noted, only the first of Pinel's three cases of mania without delirium appears to fit a modern understanding of psychopathy, and the first case involving a raving and violent individual is a marginal fit at best; thus, both the description and the illustrative cases have no bearing on the modern construct of psychopathy.

Gray (1857) was perhaps the first to connect morality, and by extension psychopathy, to Pinel, and Waughs (1941) repeated the statement in his review nearly a century later. The problem with their understandings of Pinel's earlier work, however, is that they do not appear to have read Pinel. Both Gray and Waughs relied instead on Prichard's (1835) erroneous understanding of a connection between Pinel's mania and one of his own terms, moral insanity. In addition, difficulty concerning Pinel and psychopathy may relate to his use of so-called 'moral treatment' or a more humane approach to dealing with asylum residents. In no way, however, did Pinel address the ethics or morality of his patients via any form of attitude adjustment; he simply adopted a gentler, kinder attitude toward those hospitalised with psychosocial problems by trading shackles and whips for beds and comforting words, although unpleasant forms of treatment such as ice-cold baths were employed by some moral practitioners. There does not appear to be any reason to associate psychopathy with any of Pinel's work (see also Berrios, 1999).

One early 19th century psychiatrist, or psychopathologist, who was concerned with patient ethics, or lack thereof, was Benjamin Rush. Rush, a Philadelphia physician and American patriot, focussed much of his work on what he (Rush, 1786/1839) termed "the moral faculty", or "a capacity in the human mind of distinguishing and choosing good and evil" (p. 1). Rush credited the Scottish faculty psychologists, also known as the common sense school of philosophy, for his insight. In particular, Rush (1786/1839) mentioned the work of James Beattie (1770/1772), a moral philosopher from the university in Aberdeen. Rush (1801/1812), however, developed the notion of moral faculty by pointing out that the innate faculty merely directed ethical behaviour while the conscience evaluated the nature of the acts and provided feedback. The moral faculty in most "defective" individuals was weakened rather than missing altogether and treatment was a means of strengthening the faculty. Interestingly, despite being described recently as the first to attribute criminology to a natural phenomenon within the domain of science and psychiatry rather than theology (Rafter, 2004), Rush is seldom connected to the emergence of the notion of psychopathy. When he is mentioned, any description is brief and incomplete (e. g., Arrigo and Shipley, 2001). This may be due in part to Rush's anticipation of and embrace by the phrenology movement (see forward material in Rush, 1786/1839). Even by the end of the 19th century, despite some contributions to a fuller understanding of brain specialisation, phrenology was a discredited science. The rejection was due in part to a lack of interest in the Scottish idea of innate mental faculties, although the Scots avoided the materialism of the later phrenologists by locating faculties in mind rather than brain. The real downfall of mental faculties came with the extension of phrenological theory that viewed mental faculties, such as morality or faculties such as destructiveness, as expressed in the cranial surface (see Gall, 1835). No doubt faculties and "head-lumps" were not proper grounds for the origins of psychopathy if a respectable ancestry is desired. A more respectable origin was found in the work of the renowned doctor and nosologist, James Prichard.

Prichard and Moral Insanity

James Cowles Prichard, who was active in the early to mid 1800s, was an English physician with a keen interest in medical and, in particular, psychiatric categorisation or nosology. Prichard was exposed to Scottish faculty psychology during his years of medical training at Edinburgh. Like the Scots and in opposition to materialism, his approach to psychopathology has been described as "anti-phrenological" (Augstein, 1996, p. 313). He was responsible for an early attempt to categorise psychiatric disorders (Prichard, 1835), especially ones relevant to English common law (Prichard, 1842), that included the controversial notion of moral insanity.

For Prichard (1842), moral insanity referred to "a disorder which affects only the feelings and affections, or what are termed the moral powers of the mind, in contradistinction to the powers of the understanding or intellect" (p. 19). The choice of "moral" can now be seen as unfortunate given its common meaning, even at the time (Johnson, 1768/1838), of an understanding of correct or acceptable behaviour. According to Prichard, the disorder simply pointed to the affective basis of psychological disturbance versus an intellectual basis of disorders. Berrios (1999) has interpreted it to mean psychological in a broad sense but, whatever meaning he intended, Prichard was not concerned with morality or right versus wrong. He merely proposed what we might call now mood disorders, as opposed to thought disorders, although such a distinction is somewhat simplistic. While moral insanity may produce criminal acts like assault and arson, there is no ethical connotation for Prichard, simply an attempt to expand psychiatric nosology.

Unfortunately, Prichard's attempt to coin a specialised term by employing one used differently in common parlance sparked more than a half century of debate, confusion, and controversy (Waughs, 1941; Werlinder, 1978). According to Waughs (1941), "so much time was soon spent on debating whether or not it existed that no attempt was made to study the disease entity itself" (p. 334). One lengthy debate that occurred in the United States throughout the middle of the 1800s involved two well-known psychiatric specialists, Isaac Ray and David Gray.

Ray (1839/1962), besides consistently misspelling Prichard's name, missed the point of Prichard's moral insanity diagnostic category. He separated it from what he called "affective insanity", a notion that pointed to mood disorders which seems to be exactly what Prichard was aiming for. Instead, Ray preferred the term "moral mania", and he linked it to an inborn inability to understand right from wrong or good from evil. His misunderstanding may be due to his preference for Gall's (1835) view of the brain and human functioning, a materialistic and a categorical understanding. Ray (1861) defended his understanding of moral insanity, truly a disease from his perspective, against many detractors including Gray (1857). Ray's arguments, however voluminous, do appear a little thin at times. He asserted, for instance, that no one would or should consider such capable doctors like Pinel and Prichard as supporting "a doctrine destitute of foundation and dangerous to society" (p. 113). Gray (1857), on the other hand, was unencumbered by the phrenologist's views of criminal behaviour, although materialistic enough to believe that all psychopathology was the result of some brain disease, many of which were simply unknown in the mid-1800s (c.f.,

Waldinger, 1979). As mentioned above, Gray was under the mistaken belief that Prichard was concerned with ethics and that he would "take the guilt out of sin, and convert crime into innocence" (p. 322). He argued that moral insanity was "elastic enough, if well stretched, to cover every possible shade and degree of criminality" (p. 322). He rejected it as a psychiatric or a medical condition pending empirical evidence, no doubt a prudent position. Apparently as a result of his stance, Gray was a frequent expert witness for the prosecution over decades that resulted in executions of individuals who had pled not guilty by reason of insanity (Waldinger, 1979).

Certainly some medical specialists, including prominent psychiatrists of the 19th century, were confused enough by Prichard's term, or persuaded that he was indeed suggesting a disease affecting morality, that they used it to refer to some form of ethical defect in their patients (e.g., Savage, 1881). Such use, however, was a minority understanding of moral insanity and, by the end of the 19th C the term had been eliminated from most psychiatric texts and nosologies. Various early criminologists were able to embrace moral insanity, or at least their idiosyncratic interpretations of it. The Italian Lombroso (1911), for example, saw a parallel between moral insanity and his idea of "born criminality", or the individual who had clear physical markers of an underlying, congenital condition that expressed itself as in a propensity to commit antisocial acts. Lombroso did not always maintain this connection in his work on the basis of criminality (see Werlinder, 1978, for details) but, for whatever reasons, he shifted his views and acknowledged the relevance of moral insanity for the field of criminology. Lombroso may have garnered widespread attention for some of his positions, but he did little to clarify or to popularise moral insanity. Indeed, he may well have added another nail to the coffin in the long run by tying it to an unknown innate cause and his idea of physical features of criminality, an approach soon to fall from favour among criminologists generally.

LATER 19TH AND EARLY 20TH CENTURY DEVELOPMENTS

The initial appearance of the term "psychopathic" appears in German psychiatry by about 1845 (Werlinder, 1978). It seems to refer to general psychological problems as opposed to any specific issue, but the notion was not well established until the work of Koch in the late 1880s. Like Prichard and other nosologists before him, Koch attempted to employ common words as specialised jargon, making his writing at times "difficult to understand"

(Gutmann, 2008, p. 208). Koch coined the term "psychopathic inferiority" to refer to a series of long-term, dysfunctional approaches to life which eventually became known as personality disorders. For Koch, although he did discuss the nature of criminal behaviour and improved legal responses to criminals, psychopathy did not refer to anything antisocial or offensive in any way, merely as a synonym for psychopathology. Although not very popular among psychiatric peers during his life, his work and terminology became popular among non-specialists (Gutmann, 2008).

One specialist, a renowned psychiatric nosologist, who did adopt some of Koch's terms and phrases, was Emil Kraepelin. Kraepelin (1907) devoted an entire chapter in his best-selling psychiatric text to "psychopathic personalities", a form of neurotic disorder that had four distinct sub-types. The first sub-type of psychopathic personality was the born criminal. Influenced by Lombroso's earlier work, Kraepelin argued that, in addition to physical stigmata, certain individuals demonstrate increasing criminality throughout life, often the function of parental alcoholism. Born criminals are selfish, cunning, deceitful, and callous. In addition, they tend to see themselves as "martyrs who are cruelly persecuted" (Kraepelin, 1907, p. 519). The "majority of 'professional criminals' originate" from this category (p. 519) according to Kraepelin. The second type of psychopathic personality is what Kraepelin termed "the unstable". This fairly large group includes individuals who are characterised by a general "weakness of will" (p. 521); they tend to be pessimistic, emotionally labile, overly sensitive, and unable to anything through to completion. The third sub-type, the morbid liars and swindlers, initially appear gifted in terms of memory and ability to learn but their "thought lacks system, order, and coherence; their judgment is immature" (p. 527). They seem to enjoy lying and, like the first group, they often run afoul of the law or they become "tramps" (p. 530). The final group of individuals with psychopathic personalities was termed pseudoquerulants, involving a form of paranoia that often takes the form of litigious behaviour to right perceived wrongs, with the exception that these individuals do not suffer from serious delusions. Although acceptance of Kraepelin's sub-groupings here was limited, the overall popularity and impact of Kraepelin's system, including psychopathic personality, are difficult to dispute (see Bentall, 2003).

Kurt Schneider was one German follower of Kraepelin who spread his mentor's views on psychiatric nosology, particularly psychopathic personality. Schneider, who became a leading figure in the Heidelberg school of psychiatry (see Janzarik, Viviani, and Berrios, 1998), was not a fan of Kraepelin's psychopathic personality sub-types but he did appreciate the connection between the personality disorder and antisocial behaviour. He developed a system involving 10 sub-types of psychopathic personality (for details, see Werlinder, 1978), where the psychopathological nature of the inherited disorder of psychopathy was maintained but the social damage caused by some afflicted individuals was considered. This emphasis was examined even further by other forensic psychiatrists in Germany, notably Birnbaum who published an "outstanding study" (Gurvitch, 1951, p. 89) of psychopathic criminals in 1914. Although Birnbaum maintained the view that psychopathic personality was not interchangeable with criminal, he argued that the character traits of psychopathy, such as excessive worry and self-preoccupation, led frequently to social conflict. Investigators elsewhere, such as Glueck (1918), were also beginning to focus on empirical studies relating psychopathic personality to criminality. Glueck's work on several hundred felons in an American prison showed that about one-fifth, typically with the highest rate of re-offence, were diagnosable as suffering from psychopathic personality.

Another American forensic mental health investigator, George Partridge, went beyond empirical contributions and offered a much more critical and trenchant analysis of the disorder known as psychopathic personality. Partridge (1928) studied forensic hospital patients, especially via their own writings, and found some common anti-social character traits but found more unique adaptations to difficult social demands and situations. Eventually, Partridge (1930) concluded that the psychiatric category of psychopathic personality was too broad and too diverse and, at any rate, what was being described is an abnormal reaction to abnormal social conditions. He preferred to use the term sociopathy, the first to do so (Werlinder, 1978), where the abnormal, anti-social responses or behaviours of some individuals were the focus rather than the individuals' character traits. Although the habitually sociopathic, or "essential sociopaths", created problems for Partridge, this rather interesting development provided those concerned about psychopathic personalities more issues to wrestle with.

Cason and Pascor (1946) presented a detailed empirical examination of 500 prisoners in a Missouri institution with a new "special unit for psychopaths" (p. 557). While the treatment impact, including unspecified psychotherapy, on offenders housed in this facility was rather disappointing according to the study authors, in part because the treatment was not mandatory, the demographic and outcome factors were rather interesting. The 500 male inmate-patients showed a remarkable lack of regard for other people's property, especially automobiles, and also seemed to engage in or at least were convicted frequently of sodomy, of course keeping in mind that homosexual acts were illegal in every U. S. state at this point. The 3 year re-offence rates of 37% seem high, although the re-offence specifics (e.g., type of offence) are not provided and even the authors conceded that "psychopaths may be bad prisoners, but the majority of them managed to stay out of trouble with the law" (p. 571). Cason (1948), in contrast to Partridge's views on sociopathy, believed that psychopathy involves a lack of "control of primitive antisocial behavior" (p. 297). He presented a rather general analysis of the traits, drives, and behaviours (e.g., selfishness, anger, jealousy) that psychopaths possess largely due to some innate yet non-specific reasons.

Sometimes it is instructive to examine what does not appear, versus what is being discussed, in a literature at a particular time and place. The latter 19th and early 20th centuries were noteworthy for increasing psychiatric nosologies, such as Kraepelin's work, but also for critique of such nosologies. The eminent English psychiatrist Henry Maudsley (1874/1885), for example, was very cautious in his book on criminal responsibility to avoid dealing with problems associated with moral insanity, which he did not accept as a long-term or chronic condition. Instead, he employed terms like moral feelings, moral senses, or emotions when referring to internal influences on criminal acts. Also, Hans Gross (1897/1911), who was a German expert in jurisprudence, wrote perhaps the first textbook in forensic psychology. In it he avoided discussions of moral insanity and related terminology altogether while examining the causes of criminal behaviour. If moral insanity, which to reiterate was not a forerunner of the modern understanding of psychopathy, had run its course by the end of the 19th century, other constructs like psychopathic personality and sociopathy were certainly on the rise by the middle of the 20th century.

CLECKLEY AND HIS LEGACY

If only notoriety and widespread appeal of work are considered, Hervey Cleckley is certainly one of the most significant contributors to the modern understanding of psychopathy. Cleckley, an American psychiatrist, studied and commented on psychopathy from the standpoint of a practising clinician and his first book (Cleckley, 1941) involved several dozen detailed case studies of the "so-called psychopathic personality". Although not the first to do so, Cleckley brought a neo-Freudian perspective to his study and therapy, despite his reservations about the effectiveness of psychoanalysis—really, any form of psychotherapy—in the treatment of psychopathy. He also included female patients among his cases, contrary to many other investigators, although admittedly relatively few in the first edition of his most famous book.

Faced with what he believed to be a serious disorder of an unknown biogenesis, Cleckley (1941, 1975) spent much of his effort attempting to understand and to elaborate on what, for him, were the essential characteristics of psychopathy. This was a simpler task for Cleckley than others before because, as noted by Werlinder (1978), he assumed that most clinicians have a common and clear understanding of the disorder. Cleckley (1941) described 21 basic characteristics of psychopaths initially, shortened to 14 later (Cleckley, 1959), and expanded somewhat by the time he finished his work (Cleckley, 1975). Some of his initial characteristics involved guesses, and not very educated ones, about the nature of the causes of psychopathic personality, which were unknown and genetic, and they stood out as odd in contrast to the other features described. Whatever the exact number and nature of these dysfunctional traits or character defects, the core of Cleckley's description remained relatively constant. He saw the psychopath as an antisocial or at least asocial loner, someone completely self-preoccupied and totally unconcerned about the harm that they may inflict on others in the pursuit of their own interests, although he did not believe that they had an overall or coherent life plan. They possessed superficial charm in order to manipulate others but generally lacked any real social intelligence or ability to learn from their mistakes at all. Psychopaths lie constantly to those around them in order to manipulate or manage impressions; indeed, Cleckley went so far as to state that they lack the ability to perceive the difference between truth and falsehood. They lack any sense of responsibility and sense of guilt, lacking an ability to accept any blame for their own actions. In short, the psychopath is a manipulative, dissembling, self-absorbed and possibly dangerous individual, maybe interesting and pleasant to be around but only briefly. Cleckley did not equate psychopathic personality and criminality except to suggest that crime and subsequent punishment for that matter meant nothing to a psychopath—crime was simply an expedient means to an end and one that was employed often by psychopaths.

Interestingly, although he did make an effort to include women among his cases and in his discussions, the case studies of females in Cleckley's (1941) early work seem very different from the cases involving males. As opposed to the wild, aggressive, even violent and dangerous men, the women described by Cleckley appear similar to each other in that they are diffident, sexually promiscuous, and lacking direction yet they are not antisocial law-breakers like the men. They come across more as moral offenders than legal offenders and, due to a lack of any real discussion of differences between male and female psychopaths, the reader is left to wonder if Cleckley's general observations and comments apply more to men than women.

One contemporary and colleague of Cleckley was Robert Lindner. Lindner (1944/2003) shared Cleckley's psychoanalytic orientation although he was much more optimistic about the efficacy of psychoanalysis, especially hypnoanalysis, in the treatment of psychopathy than was Cleckley. Lindner's first and perhaps most important book was a treatment report of a male client, a "criminal psychopath". Throughout this detailed account of psychoanalysis-inspired therapy Lindner showed how the defences of a serious psychopath could be breached and they could be treated successfully. Whether he was successful in convincing fellow therapists is moot but Lindner apparently did succeed in convincing Hollywood that psychopaths were a good focus for movies when a Hollywood production based loosely on Lindner (1944/2003) came out in the 1950s starring James Dean.

Cleckley's impact on mental health professionals went well beyond U. S. colleagues like Lindner. International clinicians and researchers began to ponder and to research the nature and the origins of psychopathy following Cleckley's publications. Hare (1970), a psychologist at the University of British Columbia in Canada, adopted and developed Cleckley's approach. Although he avoided psychoanalytic interpretation, Hare (1970) did accept many of Cleckley's psychopathic characteristics. Hare explored the maturational lag hypothesis in his early investigations into the development of psychopathy. This hypothesis, pointing to a late maturational point for the brain function of individuals suffering from a psychopathic condition, did appear to receive initial confirmation from studies examining brain waves of individuals considered psychopathic although support, especially later, was limited. More recently, Patrick (2003) argued that Cleckley could serve as a guide to psychopathy research and that more serious consideration of Cleckley's ideas and case descriptions would move psychopathy studies in more productive directions.

RECENT DEVELOPMENTS

Since the mid-1950s, the number of researchers and clinicians who have embraced the notion of psychopathy, especially in forensic psychiatry and psychology, have increased dramatically. This increase may be attributable to a number of factors.

The American Psychiatric Association through its series *Diagnostic and Statistical Manual of Mental Disorders (DSM)* has expanded the acceptance of the notion of psychopathic personality; unfortunately, it has not necessarily clarified our understanding of the term. The first version of the *DSM* (APA, 1952) included "sociopathic personality disturbance" under the category of personality disorder, which were described as "developmental defects or pathological trends in personality structure... manifested by a lifelong pattern of action or behavior, rather than by mental or emotional symptoms" (p. 34). Thus, while the Association appeared to be adopting Partridge's (1930) terminology, the former idea of psychopathic personality seemed at the core of the category. Adding to the confusion were the sub-types of sociopathy, including "antisocial reaction" and "sexual deviation", that were in general described as a lack "of conformity with the prevailing cultural milieu" (p. 38). Subsequent editions of the *DSM* eliminated the term "sociopathy", settling instead on "antisocial personality disorder" in the most recent version of the manual (APA, 2000). While this nomenclature may eliminate some internal inconsistency, pointing to the defective traits of individuals that produce antisocial behaviour, it is distinctive from psychopathy and even sociopathy insofar as its focus is criminal behaviour. While the differences may appear small, they exist nonetheless, and some efforts (e.g., Hare, Hart, and Harpur, 1991) have been made to resolve some of the differences among the various terms that appear similar. Any reader interested in a detailed account of changes in the psychiatric understanding of antisocial personality disorder over the past 50 years should consult Pickersgill (2010).

The World Health Organisation's (WHO, 2004) *International Statistical Classification of Diseases and Related Health Problems—10th Revision* (*ICD-10*) has gone through various changes over the years like the DSM. In past years it employed "sociopathic personality" but *ICD-10* now employs a diagnosis nearly identical to antisocial personality disorder, dissocial personality disorder, in its chapter on mental and behavioural disorders. Similar to antisocial personality disorder, the dissocial disorder involves a number of criteria indicative of a lack of regard for other individuals. These diagnostic criteria include a lack of concern for others' feelings, a low frustration tolerance with likelihood to employ aggression or violence, a tendency to blame others, and a lack of capacity to experience guilt. Clearly, like antisocial personality disorder, dissocial personality disorder emphasizes antisocial behaviour related to problems with the law and, as such, differs somewhat from the notion of psychopathy. In terms of differences, dissocial subsumes antisocial and other personality disorders (e.g., asocial) in the *ICD-*

10 listing, and it seems to focus more on affective deficits than actual antisocial behaviour (for a detailed discussion, see Ogloff, 2006).

Beyond recent organisational developments, a number of theorists and clinicians presented various ideas and studies over the past half century. Sociological perspectives played a role in some research. Gough (1948), for example, argued for a view of the psychopath as deficient in role-playing. From Gough's social-psychological foundation, psychopaths are unable to adopt the role of the other in a significant way and hence are unable to understand and to relate meaningfully to social actors. According to Gough, this helps to explain psychopaths' social and legal conflicts as well as their limited emotional experiences; unfortunately, he ignored the charm and social skills, however superficial, that such individuals use as a means of duping and using others. Robins (1966), too, relied on a sociological perspective, no doubt due to her doctoral level training in sociology, to study 100s of high-risk children. After considering many demographic and psychiatric variables possibly related to sociopathy, Robins showed that there were a number of childhood factors (e. g., parental alcoholism, parental display of sociopathic characteristics) that determined subsequent sociopathic behaviour in target children. Given her sociological background, rather strangely Robins emphasised the biogenesis of her findings throughout her discussions. More recently, Robins has been involved in a number of large-scale social epidemiological studies of psychopathy and its variants. Robins and Price (1991), for example, examined conduct disorders among young people in the United States and, besides showing an increase in such problems over several decades, they showed a clear link between conduct disorders and antisocial personality disorder. As always, Robins emphasized the importance of early intervention and even prevention in order to address more serious adult problems like antisocial behavior.

Since the 1980s, there have been a number of attempts to present a social psychological view of psychopathy. Smith (1984, 1999) presented a rather interesting social psychological explanation of psychopathy. Smith (1984) argued that insofar as Western societies seem to promote values such as "watch out for number one" and "do your own thing" an individual labelled psychopathic has merely acquired via learning the values of the mainstream culture and they are simply a "heavily socialized, not antisocial personality" (p. 193). In a sense the psychopath, at least according to Smith, has a bright future in an increasingly individualistic and competitive West so long as they have opportunities to channel antisocial activities into more acceptable forms. Smith (1999) suggested a form of "entrepreneurial therapy" to turn, for example, drug dealers into captains of innovation and pro-social advancers of the marketplace. Levenson (1992), too, saw the need for a social learning-based theoretical account of psychopathy, and he described psychopathy as a philosophy of life or moral stance based on social experience and early life experience. Like Smith, by avoiding a pathological perspective, he suggested how psychopaths could be re-oriented or have their skills re-directed toward more prosocial activities.

In addition to Robins, a number of contemporary researchers considered and studied developmental aspects of psychopathy in detail. McCord and McCord (1956, 1964), a husband and wife research team from the United States, argued for a rather nuanced view of psychopathy, especially when children and adolescents are concerned. They saw psychopathy as a dimensional versus a categorical entity ranging from relatively minor social maladjustment to persistent antisocial involvement. From their perspective, the term psychopath should be reserved for the few, hardened, serious individuals. McCord and McCord (1964) discussed not only their theory of psychopathic personality, which appeared shaped by Cleckley, as well as the prospects for treatment. Perhaps not surprisingly, they were much more optimistic about treatment prospects than most of their forerunners, most of whom are clearly in the categorical camp, especially in light of the results from training facilities targeting at-risk youth.

Karpman (1947a, 1947b), as well, was interested in the genesis of psychopathy, especially what he termed primary or essential psychopathy in contrast to secondary or symptomatic psychopathy (Karpman, 1947b). The primary psychopath, according to Karpman (1947b), is the only true psychopath in that they do not respond to treatment because of the depth of the pathology, although "the constitutional angle of the evil" (p. 220) is not well understood. Secondary psychopaths are more responsive to treatment because their pathology is related to an environmentally-produced character flaw. Primary psychopathy is comprised of two sub-types, the aggressive predatory type and the passive parasitic type. Both prey on others in that they care only for their own needs, but the aggressive predator is much more active in terms of their search for victims, usually expending much energy, while the passive parasitic type tends to engage in lethargic "sponging" (p. 219). From his psychoanalytic perspective, primary psychopaths, although only a small minority of individuals described as psychopathic, were the most puzzling despite some understanding of their psychogenesis (e. g., no resolution of Oedipal Complex, no insight developed).

An influential psychologist based in England, Hans Eysenck, has embraced psychopathy and made it part, admittedly a minor part, of his personality theory. Eysenck (1964) has written on the nature of criminality and attempted to explain it in terms of his biological view of human personality. According to Eysenck, psychopaths are neurotic extraverts, inotherwords they score high on the dimensions of extraversion and neuroticism, two basic dimensions that comprise personality. Extraverts tend to be outgoing stimulus seekers because of cortical inhibition, which refers to relatively little activity in the cerebral cortex due to stimulation, while neurotics tend to be emotionally labile. The problem with this formulation, aside from the broader issue of lack of empirical support for Eysenck's biological theory, is that an essential element of psychopathy and related terms is that those diagnosed as psychopathic, sociopathic, etc. show little emotional expression. Although the original formulation was later amended (Eysenck, 1977) to include a third dimension, psychoticism or "weak-mindedness" which refers to a tendency to lack control over one's thoughts, the basic incompatibility with common understandings of psychopathy, at least since Cleckley, remained in Eysenck's work. It is interesting to note Eysenck's connection at the University of London through his mentors in psychology and the eugenics movement, a movement that is associated with the "invention" of innate criminality (Rafter, 1997a).

One of the most prolific current contributors to psychopathy research and theory is Robert Hare. Hare has published dozens of studies (for a review, see Hare and Neumann, 2008), including many empirical studies of his own contribution to the assessment of psychopathy, the Psychopathy Checklist—Revised (PCL-R). In forensic settings the PCL-R has become the most validated assessment technique concerned with psychopathy (for a detailed review of PCL-R and its development, see Lynam and Gudonis, 2005). Although the PCL-R has become the most popular psychopathy assessment, there are other measures available such as the Psychopathic Personality Inventory (PPI; Lilienfeld and Andrews, 1996), and it has spurred critics to propose "purified" measures of psychopathy (Cook, Michie, Hart, and Clark, 2004). It has also raised various legal concerns such as its use as a predictive device in some courtroom (DeMatteo and Edens, 2006). Although very clearly influenced by the work of Cleckley (see Hare, 1970), it would be unfair to describe Hare as a mere Cleckleyan given that he has acknowledged that his work reflects the influences of other clinicians such as the McCords (Hare and Neumann, 2008). Neo-Cleckleyan is perhaps a better descriptor.

Hare's model of psychopathy is more complex than many others, certainly when compared to Cleckley's view. He has proposed two separate factors, an affective or interpersonal factor made up of numerous characteristics (e.g., glibness, shallow affect, lack of empathy) and a social deviance factor (e.g., impulsivity, criminal versatility, parasitic lifestyle). As well, each of the two factors has two facets. Like Cleckley, Hare (1993) emphasized that, while psychopaths may be incarcerated for some of their criminal activities, psychopathy is not synonymous with criminality. For Hare (1996), psychopaths do comprise 15-25% of prison populations, and roughly 1% of the general population, but they are represented in business, politics, and other non-criminal pursuits. Unfortunately, this position drives a further wedge between psychopathy and related notions like antisocial personality disorder, a gap that Hare has attempted to bridge (Hare et al., 1991), because fewer than a quarter of incarcerated offenders are classified as psychopathic versus more than three-quarters as antisocial personality disordered (Ogloff, 2006; Shipley and Arrigo, 2001). This broader view of psychopathy has been emphasised by Hare and colleagues (e.g., Babiak and Hare, 2006) who have discussed the business and political activities of so-called psychopaths.

There has been an apparent increase in the number of publications critical of psychopathy and related terms in recent years. As shown in the preceeding pages, this is not new but it is worth noting as perhaps indicative of a trend. The recommendations made by some critics recently have been quite extreme yet perhaps overdue and certainly welcome.

The notion of psychopathic personality, and closely related notions like antisocial personality disorder, has been the brunt of many conceptual critiques. Lewis (1973), in a very wide-ranging historical review and critique of the psychopathic personality, pointed out the rather broad and shifting understandings of the category in addition to the limited research. His recommendation was to do more research while Gunn and Robertson (1976), who provided some research on the trait-characteristic correspondence of the diagnosis of psychopathic personality, argued that the diagnosis was being applied far too often and too loosely, and that it should be restricted. Blackburn (1988), citing lack of homogeniety in the construct, recommended that the term be discarded entirely by mental health professionals, a suggestion endorsed for psychopathy by Gendreau, Goggin, and Smith (2002). Horley (2011) also recommended discarding psychopathy because of concerns about the negative effects of labelling which appear to carry personal and social consequences. Skeen et al. (2003) did not recommend dispensing with psychopathy entirely but they did argue that psychopathy is not the unitary entity that it is presumed to be, and they suggested that multiple psychopathies would improve treatment effectiveness.

Sociopathy, too, has come under scrutiny by Barocas (1970) who suggested that, while little appears to be known about sociopathy, any theory that points to disease is not viable. The North American or Cleckleyan version of psychopathy has come in for some criticism as well. Walters (2004), for example, questioned the appropriateness of a broad view of psychopathy or antisocial personality disorder as an explanation of all crime. Federman, Holmes, and Jacob (2009) examined psychopathy from a Foucaultian perspective and concluded that "it would be better for everyone if the word showed up more often in Hollywood and less in the halls of science" (p. 57). Unfortunately, the halls of science are too often interpreted and reflected through the eyes of Hollywood.

Summary and Conclusion

There have been many attempts, often relying on the statements of prior writers, to tie psychopathy and related terms to the psychiatry and psychopathology of the early 1800s. There is, however, no evidence to suggest that the modern understandings of psychopathy, sociopathy, psychopathic personality, or antisocial personality disorder have any roots in the work of the usual candidates, Pinel and Prichard. Pinel's mania without delusion and Prichard's moral insanity do not have any clear relationships with psychopathy or related diagnoses except superficial ones, and these no doubt have deceived many previous mental health professionals curious about the history of psychopathy. As Berrios (1999) and Whitlock (1982) have pointed out, it is simply a matter of returning to the original sources and reading diagnostic descriptions and representative cases in order to see that mania without delusions and moral insanity bear no resemblance to psychopathy, psychopathic personality, or any such terms.

Without question, psychiatrists and physicians such as Rush and Gall did consider the nature and breakdown of posited entities such as a moral faculty in the commission of illegal acts or antisocial behaviour, but the connection, say, between a destructiveness faculty located in the brain above the right orbital socket is a far cry from the modern North American psychopathy construct and, besides, almost no one is prepared to claim such connections. The term psychopathy only appears in any signifcant manner very late in the

19th century in the work of Koch and then only as a synonym for psychopathology. There is no link to criminal or antisocial activity.

The early decades of the 20th century, through the work of Kraepelin and Schneider, do see some formulations that begin to resemble the psychopath of the early 21st century. Kraepelinian sub-types of psychopathic personality that tie "born criminality" and compulsive thievery to defective personality traits and characteristics start to look like the beginnings of the emergence of psychopathic man, but only loosely. It is not until Partridge's work on sociopathic personality, and a decade later the case studies and theory of Cleckley, that antisocial behaviour and internal dynamics that resemble more closely the modern psychopath truly emerge. More than any other single individual, Cleckley shaped very much the modern psychopath not only directly but also indirectly through influence on the work of the McCords and Hare.

The proliferation of terminology related to psychopathy over the past several decades is obvious, as is the imprecision of each of the terms. The confusion, professional and otherwise, caused by the many unclear terms is obvious and, despite the claims of some writers (e. g., Shipley and Arrigo, 2001) to remedy the confusion, it persists today. In general, all of the constructs seem to include some sort of underlying yet indeterminant biogenetic cause or causes although there are individual writers who seem to favour more social factors. It is unfortunate that there seems to be no evidence to support positions that emphasise sociogenesis, but it is equally unfortunate for those who favour biogenesis that there is no real support here either despite some very testable hypotheses (Eysenck, 1964; Hare, 1970).

The wooliness that continues to surround psychopathy, sociopathy, antisocial personality disorder, and the rest of these so-called disorders seems unacceptable. Adherence to such problematic notions seems to defy logic, although there are perhaps various ways to interpret it. Rafter (1997b) has offered an intriguing suggestion to explain the imprecision. She argued that, at least with respect to American criminology, the imprecision in the meaning of psychopathy is precisely why it was used by criminologists. Psychopaths, on the border of normal and abnormal, are misfits or "others" who difference is obvious but impossible to describe precisely or in terms that all would agree, although all would agree that they exist. In this way, psychopathy serves for Rafter as a metaphor for "those who are not like us" (p. 250), and the very vagueness of the metaphor makes it a powerful social adhesive (i.e., we interpret the metaphor as we will but assume that everyone shares our interpretation). An alternative explanation may involve monster making and the view of psychopaths as modern monsters (Horley, 2008). We create monsters for many reasons, but they all serve to warn about possible dangers, whether the dangers concern walking in the woods at night or sailing in a certain part of the sea. In the case of psychopathy, the warning points clearly at the danger of keeping company with certain people. Monsters are rarely understood but they are feared, and the only way to properly deal with them to kill or to isolate them. Psychopaths are modern monsters insofar as they may have no fangs or are not necessarily bloodthirsty killers, but they are unpleasant if not dangerous to be around. They are also a threat to well-meaning psychotherapists who take them on as clients, only to waste time and ultimately end up at the end of a frivolous lawsuit or criminal inquiry. Psychopaths need to be identified, isolated, and avoided.

Whatever the reason or reasons behind the current lack of clarity surrounding psychopathy and all its variants, a solution to the problem is required. Moral judgments concealed in technical jargon, especially unclear and inconsistent terminology, should not be tolerated by anyone least of all professionals who would have the public believe that they are ultimately concerned about their clients' welfare. Perhaps Blackburn's (1988) call for the abandonment of psychopathic personality should be expanded to include psychopathy, sociopathy, and all related terms. Individuals who are facing such labels in the therapy room or the courtroom may well thank us for eliminating such significant and unnecessary hurdles to their recovery and rehabilitation or continued life.

REFERENCES

American Psychiatric Association. (2000). *Diagnostic and statistical manual of mental disorders—Text revision (4th Edition)*. Washington: Author.

American Psychiatric Association. (1952). *Diagnostic and statistical manual of mental disorders.* Washington: Author.

Arrigo B.A., and Shipley S. (2001). The confusion over psychopathy: Historical considerations. *International Journal of Offender Therapy and Comparative Criminology, 45,* 325-344.

Augstein, H. F. (1996). .J C Prichard's concept of moral insanity—A medical theory of the corruption of human nature. *Medical History, 40*, 311-343.

Babiak, P., and Hare, R. D. (2006). *Snakes in suits: When psychopaths go to work.* New York: HarperBusiness.

Barocas, R. (1970). Some problems in the conception of sociopathy. *Psychiatric Quarterly, 44*, 674-686.

Beattie, J. (1772). *An essay on the nature and immutability of truth, in opposition to sophistry and scepticism (3rd Edition)*. Edinburgh: Kincaid, Creech, and Bell. (Original work published 1770.)

Bentall, R. P. (2003). *Madness explained: Psychosis and human nature*. London: Penguin.

Berrios, G. E. (1999). J. C. Prichard and the concept of moral insanity. *History of Psychiatry, 10,* 111-126.

Blackburn, R. (1988). On moral judgements and personality disorders: The myth of psychopathic personality revisited. *British Journal of Psychiatry, 153*, 505-512.

Cason, H. (1948). The concept of the psychopath. *American Journal of Orthopsychiatry, 18,* 297-308.

Cason, H., and Pescor, M. J. (1946). A statistical study of 500 psychopathic prisoners. *Public Health Reports, 61,* 557-574.

Cleckley, H. (1975). *The mask of sanity: An attempt to clarify some issues about the so-called psychopathic personality (5th Edition)*. St. Louis: Mosby.

Cleckley, H. (1959). Psychopathic states. In S. Arieti (Ed), *American handbook of psychiatry (Volume 1; pp.* 567-588). New York: Basic Books.

Cleckley, H. (1941). *The mask of sanity: An attempt to clarify some issues about the so-called psychopathic personality*. St. Louis: Mosby.

Cook, D. J., Michie, C., Hart, S. D., and Clark D. A. (2004). Reconstructing psychopathy: Clarifying the significance of antisocial and socially deviant behavior in the diagnosis of psychopathic personality disorder. *Journal of Personality Disorders,18,* 337-357.

Dematteo, D., and Edens J. F. (2006). The role and relevance of the Psychopathy Checklist—Revised in court: A case law survey of U. S. courts (1991-2004). *Psychology, Public Policy, and Law, 12,* 214-241.

Edens, J. F., and Petrila, J. (2003). Legal and ethical issues in the assessment and treatment of psychopathy. In C. J. Patrick (Ed.), *Handbook of psychopathy* (pp. 573-588). New York: Guilford.

Eysenck, H. J. (1977). *Crime and personality (2nd Edition).* London: Routledge.

Eysenck, H. J. (1964). *Crime and personality*. London: Routledge and Kegan Paul. Federman, C., Holmes, D., and Jacob J. D. (2009). Deconstructing the psychopath: A critical discursive analysis. *Cultural Critique, 72,* 36-65.

Gall, F. J. (1835). *On the functions of the brain and of each of its parts.* Boston: Marsh, Capen, and Lyon.

Gendreau, P., Goggin, C., and Smith, P. (2002). Is the PCL-R really the "unparallelled" measure of offender risk? A lesson in knowledge accumulation. *Criminal Justice and Behavior, 29,* 397-426.

Glueck, B. (1918). Studies of admissions to Sing Sing. *Mental Hygiene, 2, 119*-139.

Gough, H. G. (1948). A sociological theory of psychopathy. *American Journal of Sociology, 53,* 359-366.

Gray, J. P. (1857). Moral insanity. *American Journal of Insanity, 14,* 311-322.

Gross, H. (1911). *Criminal psychology: A manual for judges, practitioners, and students.* Boston: Little, Brown, and Company. (Original work published in 1897.)

Gunn, J., and Robertson, G. (1976). Psychopathic personality: A conceptual problem. *Psychological Medicine, 6,* 631-634.

Gurvitz, M. (1951). Developments in the concept of psychopathic personality (1900- 1950). *British Journal of Delinquency, 2,* 88-102.

Gutmann, P. (2008). Julius Ludwig August Koch (1841-1908): Christian, philosopher, and psychiatrist. *History of Psychiatry, 19,* 202-214.

Hare R. D. (1996). Psychopathy: A clinical construct whose time has come. *Criminal Justice and Behavior, 23*, 25-54.

Hare R. D. (1993). *Without conscience: The disturbing world of the psychopaths among us*. New York: Guilford.

Hare R. D. (1970). *Psychopathy: Theory and research.* New York: John Wiley and Sons.

Hare R. D., Hart, S. D., and Harpur, T. J. (1991). Psychopathy and the DSM-IV criteria for antisocial personality disorder. *Journal of Abnormal Psychology, 100*, 391-398.

Hare R. D., and Neumann, C. S. (2008). Psychopathy as a clinical and empirical construct *Annual Review of Clinical Psychology, 4*, 217-246.

Horley, J. (2011). On the tyranny of professional labelling. *Psychotherapy and Politics International, 9,* 127-133.

Horley, J. (2008). *Sexual offenders: Personal construct theory and deviant sexual behaviour.* New York: Routledge.

Janzarik, W., Viviani, R., and Berrios, G. E. (1998). Jaspers, Kurt Schneider, and the Heidelberg school of psychiatry. *History of Psychiatry, 9*, 241-252.

Johnson, S. (1838). *A dictionary of the English language (3rd Edition).* Dublin: Jones (Original work published 1768).

Karpman, B. (1947). Moral agenesis: Toward the delimitation of the problem of psychopathic states. *Psychiatric Quarterly, 21,* 361-398. (a)

Karpman, B. (1947). Passive parasitic psychopathy: Toward the personality structure and psychogenesis of idiopathic psychopathy (anethopathy). *Psychoanalytic Review, 34, 102*-118, 198-222. (b)

Kraepelin, E. (1907). *Clinical psychiatry: A text-book for students and physicians.* New York: Macmillan Company.

Levenson, M. R. (1992). Rethinking psychopathy. *Theory and Psychology, 2,* 51-71.

Lewis, A. (1973). Psychopathic personality: A most elusive category. *Psychological Medicine, 4,* 133-140.

Lilienfeld, S. O., and Andrews, B. P. (1996). Development and preliminary validation of a self-report measure of psychopathic personality traits in noncriminal populations. *Journal of Personality Assessment, 66*, 488-524.

Lindner, R. M. (2003). *Rebel without a cause: The story of a criminal psychopath.* New York: Other Press. (Original work published 1944.)

Lombroso, C. (1911). *Criminal man.* New York: G. P. Putnam's Sons. Lyman, D. R., and Gudonis, L. (2005). The development of psychopathy. *Annual Review of Clinical Psychology, 1,* 381-407.

McCord, W, and McCord, J. (1964). *The psychopath: An essay on the criminal mind.* New York: Van Nostrand.

McCord, W, and McCord, J. (1956). *Psychopathy and delinquency.* New York: Grune and Stratton.

Mason, T. (2006). An archaeology of the psychopath: The medicalization of evil. In T. Mason (Ed.), *Forensic psychiatry: The influences of evil* (pp. 89-108). Totawa: Humana Press.

Maudsley, H. (1885). *Responsibility in mental disease (4th edition*). London: Kegan Paul, Trench, and Company. (Original work published 1874.)

Millon, T., Simonsen, E., and Birket-Smith, M. (1998). Historical conceptions of psychopathy in the United States and Europe. In T. Millon, E. Simonsen, M. Birket-Smith, and R. D. Davies (Eds.), *Psychopathy: Antisocial, criminal, and violent behavior* (pp. 3-31). New York: Guilford.

Ogloff, J. R.P. (2006). Psychopathy/antisocial personality disorder conundrum. *Australian and New Zealand Journal of Psychiatry, 40*, 519-528.

Patrick, C. J. (2003). Back to the future: Cleckley as a guide to the next generation of psychopathy research. In C. J. Patrick (Ed.), *Handbook of psychopathy (pp.* 605-612). New York: Guilford.

Partridge, G. E. (1930). Current conceptions of psychopathic personality. *American Journal of Psychiatry, 87*, 53-99.

Partridge, G. E. (1928). A study of 50 cases of psychopathic personality. *American Journal of Psychiatry, 84*, 953-973.

Pickersgill, M. (2010). From psyche to soma? Changing accounts of antisocial personality disorders in the *American Journal of Psychiatry*. *History of Psychiatry, 21,* 294-311.

Pinel, P. (1806). *A treatise on insanity*. Sheffield: Todd. (Original work published 1801).

Prichard, J. C. (1842). *On the different forms of insanity in relation to jurisprudence*. London: Bailliere.

Prichard, J. C. (1835). *A treatise on insanity and other disorders of the mind.* London: Sherwood, Gilbert and Piper.

Rafter, N. (2004). The unrepentant horse-slasher: Moral insanity and the origins of criminological thought. *Criminology, 42*, 979-1008.

Rafter, N. (1997). *Creating born criminals.* Urbana: University of Illinois Press. (a) Rafter, N. (1997). Psychopathy and the evolution of criminological knowledge. *Theoretical Criminology, 1*, 235-259. (b)

Ray, I. (1962). *A treatise on the medical jurisprudence of insanity*. Cambridge: Belknap Press. (Original work published 1838.)

Ray, I. (1861). An examination of the objection to the doctrine of moral insanity. *American Journal of Insanity,18,* 112-138.

Robins, L. N. (1966). *Deviant children grow up: A sociological and psychiatric study of sociopathic personality*. Baltimore: Williams and Wilkins.

Robins, L. N. and Price, R. K. (1991). Adult disorders predicted by childhood conduct problems: Results from the NIMH epidemiologic catchment area project. *Psychiatry, 54,* 116-132.

Rush, B. (1839). *An inquiry into the influence of physical causes upon the moral faculty*. Philadelphia: Haswell, Barrington and Haswell. (Original work presented 1786)

Rush, B. (1812). *Medical inquiries and observations upon the diseases of the mind.* Philadelphia: Kimber and Richardson. (Original work published 1801.)

Savage, G. H. (1881). Moral insanity. *British Journal of Psychiatry, 27,* 147-155.

Shipley, S., and Arrigo B.A. (2001). The confusion over psychopathy: Implications for forensic (correctional) practice. *International Journal of Offender Therapy and Comparative Criminology, 45,* 407-420.

Skeen, J. L., Poythress, N., Edens, J. F., Lilienfeld, S. O., and Cale, E. M. (2003). Psychopathic personality or personalities? Exploring potential variants of psychopathy and their implications for risk assessment. *Aggression and Violent Behavior, 8,* 513-546.

Smith, R. J. (1999). Psychopathic behavior and issues of treatment. *New Ideas in Psychology, 17,* 165-176.

Smith, R. J. (1984). The psychopath as moral agent. *Philosophy and Phenomenological Research, 45,* 177-193.

Temkin, O. (1946). An essay on the usefulness of medical history for medicine. *Bulletin of the History of Medicine, 19,* 9-47.

Waldinger, R. J. (1979). The sleep of reason: John P. Gray and the challenge of moral insanity. *Journal of the History of Medicine and Allied Sciences, 34,* 163-179.

Walters, G. D. (2004). The trouble with psychopathy as a general theory of crime. *International Journal of Offender Therapy and Comparative Criminology; 48,* 133-148.

Werlinder H. (1978). *Psychopathy: A history of the concepts.* Stockholm: Almquist and Wiksell.

Whitlock, F. A. (1982). A note on moral insanity and psychiatric disorders. *Psychiatric Bulletin, 6,* 57-59.

World Health Organization (2004). *International Statistical Classification of Diseases and Related Health Problems—10th Revision (2nd Edition).* Geneva: World Health Organization.

In: Born Bad? Critiques of Psychopathy
Editor: James Horley
ISBN: 978-1-62618-082-6

Chapter 3

PSYCHOPATHY'S ROLE IN THE CRIMINAL JUSTICE SYSTEM: FIVE EMPIRICAL CONTROVERSIES IN SEARCH OF ANSWERS

Glenn D. Walters[*]
Kutztown University, Kutztown, Pennsylvania

INTRODUCTION

It is often assumed that psychopathy in general and Hare's (2003) Psychopathy Checklist-Revised (PCL-R), a 20-item rating scale designed to measure psychopathy, in particular have a great deal to offer the criminal justice system. Hare (1998) has consistently characterized psychopathy as "the single most important clinical construct in the criminal justice system" (p. 99). More recently, he and several colleagues have made mention of the "very large literature on the important role of psychopathy in the criminal justice system" which has grown up around the PCL-R (Babiak, Neumann, and Hare, 2010, p. 174). In a paper published nearly two decades ago, Salekin et al. (1996) described Hare's (2003) Psychopathy Checklist-Revised (PCL-R) as "unparalleled…for making risk assessments with white male inmates" (p. 211). Echoing these sentiments in a recent interview on national radio, Richards (2011) states that the "PCL-R is the most reliable tool the criminal

[*] Address all correspondence to Glenn D. Walters, Department of Criminal Justice, Kutztown University, Kutztown, Pennsylvania 18530; e-mail: walters@kutztown.edu

justice system has to identify chronic, pathologic offenders [because] it enables corrections systems to make better decisions about resource allocation and interventions." Such strong statements require empirical verification.

I tackled this issue once before, around ten years ago, in a paper published in the *International Journal of Offender Therapy and Comparative Criminology* entitled "The trouble with psychopathy as a general theory of crime" (Walters, 2004). In that paper, I assessed the relevance of the psychopathy construct to the criminal justice system using six criteria of a good theory: comprehensiveness, parsimony, fruitfulness, precision, internal consistency, and empirical validity. Based on my review of the literature, I gave psychopathy high marks on two of the six criteria, fruitfulness and parsimony, and low marks on three other criteria, comprehensiveness, precision, and internal consistency. Based on the available literature I was unable to come to a conclusion on the empirical validity of the psychopathy construct for the purpose of creating a general theory of crime. In the years since, several psychopathy-oriented controversies have arisen. An examination of these controversies may help answer the question of whether there is empirical support for the relevance of psychopathy and the PCL-R to crime and the criminal justice system.

Empirical Controversy #1: Can Psychopathy be Reliability Measured in Juveniles?

Before delving into the question of whether it is possible to reliably assess psychopathy in juveniles, adult data on the inter-rater reliability of the most popular measure of psychopathy (i.e., the PCL-R) will be examined. The inter-rater reliability (consistency of scores between two or more raters) of the PCL-R is strong for ratings made in research settings. The PCL-R manual reports single rater (absolute agreement) intra-class correlation coefficients for the PCL-R total, factor, and facet scores of .86-.94, .75-.92, and .67-.89, respectively, in research analyses conducted with a single interview (Hare, 2003). When inter-rater reliability is assessed in a clinical context with each rater conducting separate interviews, the inter-rater reliability of the PCL-R is less impressive. Murrie et al. (2009) compared independent PCL-R evaluations for 35 Sexually Violent Predator (SVP) civil commitment cases and obtained a total PCL-R intra-class correlation coefficient of .42 for psychologists working on opposing sides (petitioner and respondent) and an intra-class correlation coefficient of .47 for psychologists working on the same side (petitioner). Analyzing PCL-R results attained by opposing psychologists in 15 Canadian case law reports, Lloyd, Clark, and Forth (2011) witnessed a level of inter-rater reliability (intra-class correlation coefficient = .67) that was higher than the estimates obtained by Murrie et al. (2009) but lower than those reported in the PCL-R manual. Edens, Boccaccini, and Johnson (2010) analyzed Factors 1 (affective-interpersonal aspects of psychopathy) and 2 (antisocial-lifestyle aspects of psychopathy) of the PCL-R separately in a study comparing independent PCL-R evaluations on 20 sex offenders. The results revealed that Factor 2 had higher inter-rater reliability (intra-class correlation coefficient = .56) than Factor 1 (intra-class correlation coefficient = .16).

Lynam (1997, 1998) contends that psychopathy can be reliably diagnosed in children and adolescents because it is a developmental construct with continuity from childhood to adulthood. A modified version of the 20-item PCL-R, the Psychopathy Checklist: Youth Version (PCL:YV: Forth, Kosson, and Hare, 2003), has been used to support the reliability and validity of measured psychopathy in individuals between the ages of 12 and 18 (Olver et al., 2010). Regardless of how well the youth version of the Psychopathy Checklist performs, however, application of the psychopathy construct to juveniles is a highly controversial topic and there are at least four potential problems with extending the psychopathy construct to youth. First, all major measures of psychopathy were originally designed for adults, normally adult incarcerated offenders, and some have been extended to youth. Frick and Marsee (2006) contend that the question of whether these methods are appropriate for use with children and adolescents has been largely ignored by researchers. Second, there is very limited information on the long-term stability of these psychopathy measures (Caufman and Skeem, 2003). Third, there is concern that some of the traits used to assess psychopathy in adults (e.g., egocentricity, irresponsibility, impulsivity) may be normative and transient (Seagreave and Grisso, 2002) in juveniles and that application of the psychopathy construct to youth may pathologize normal adolescent behavior. Fourth, applying the psychopathy construct to non-adults could stigmatize youth, decrease their opportunities for treatment, and make it more likely that their cases will be transferred to adult court (Edens, Guy, and Fernandez, 2003).

Reliability (consistency of scores over time, across raters, or within a scale), being a prerequisite for validity (ability of a test to measure what it is supposed to measure), places an upper limit on validity. If the reliability of an instrument is weak then its validity will be weak as well. A measure that achieves modest inter-rater reliability (intra-class correlation coefficient = .16 to .67) in clinical settings will struggle to achieve minimal levels of clinical utility and validity. A construct developed on adults cannot be assumed to be applicable to juveniles without strong empirical backing. The modest reliability of the PCL-R in clinical situations and the uncertain reliability and stability of the psychopathy construct in youth brings into serious question the validity and utility of both the PCL-R and psychopathy construct. Continued research is required to determine the degree to which the less than optimal reliability of the PCL-R limits the measure's validity and the extent to which the psychopathy construct generalizes to children and adolescents who find themselves in trouble with the law.

EMPIRICAL CONTROVERSY #2: DOES PSYCHOPATHY FORM A QUALITATIVELY DISTINCT CATEGORY?

Harris, Rice, and Quinsey (1994) used Meehl's (1995, 2004) taxometric method to assess the latent structure of PCL-R-measured psychopathy in a group of 653 mentally disturbed prison inmates. Using dichotomous PCL-R items (present-absent)[1] as indicators and a single taxometric procedure (maximum covariance), Harris and colleagues uncovered what they believed was a taxon (distinct group or category) in PCL-R-measured psychopathy. When items from Factors 1 and 2 were analyzed separately, however, only Factor 2 showed evidence of categorical latent structure. The personality features assessed by Factor 1 unexpectedly failed to produce a taxon. As an initial attempt to assess the latent structure of psychopathy, the Harris et al. (1994) study suffered from several noteworthy conceptual and methodological flaws. First, taxometrics require the use of quasi-continuous indicators, which, according to the results of a recent Monte Carlo analysis (Walters and Ruscio, 2009), are composed of four or more ordered categories. The dichotomous indicators in the Harris et al. (1994) study clearly do not qualify as quasi-continuous. Second, taxometrics rests on the principle of consistency testing (congruence of results across several different non-redundant procedures). Harris et al. (1994) used only one of three validated indices (i.e., maximum covariance) and paired this with two unvalidated indices (i.e., Base Rate Consistency, Bayesian analysis: Ruscio, Haslam, and Ruscio, 2006) and so failed to take advantage of consistency testing. Finally, Ruscio et al.'s (2006) comparative curve approach should be employed, particularly with skewed and non-normal indicators, to avoid making erroneous inferences about curve shape. Harris et al. (1994) did not use this approach because it was not available in 1994 and so some of their interpretations of the observed patterns may have been in error.

Table 1 provides a breakdown of taxometric research on the latent structure of psychopathy using indicators from the PCL-R, a PCL-R derivative (PCL:SV, PCL:YV), or one of the self-report measures that have been developed to assess psychopathy (Antisocial Process Screening Device [APSD: Frick and Hare, 2001], Levenson Self-Report Psychopathy scale [LSRP: Levenson, Kiehl, and Fritzpatrick, 1995], Psychopathic Personality Inventory [, PPI: Lilienfeld and Andrews, 1996]). The results tend to favor a dimensional interpretation of the latent structure of psychopathy. For one, studies supporting a dimensional interpretation of the latent structure of psychopathy outnumber studies supporting a categorical interpretation, nearly two to one. For another, all but one of the five categorical-leaning studies suffered from at least one of the three methodological flaws referenced earlier with respect to the Harris et al. (1994) study (i.e., failure to use quasi-continuous indicators, failure to implement consistency testing, failure to employ Ruscio et al.'s (2006) comparison curve approach), whereas none of the nine dimensional-leaning studies suffered from a single one of these flaws. Moreover, the one categorical-leaning study that used quasi-continuous indicators, consistency testing, and Ruscio et al.'s (2006) comparison curve approach (i.e., Vasey et al., 2005) presents several additional methodological problems. Two methodological limitations in particular, were Vasey et al.'s (2005) failure to represent multiple aspects of a construct (psychopathy) in the indicators—using instead, multiple measures of the same aspect—and admixing samples—in this case, a community sample and an adjudicated sample—thereby increasing the odds of observing a pseudotaxon (Murrie et al., 2007).

What does it mean that psychopathy is probably dimensional? First of all, it means that individual differences in psychopathy are more a matter of degree (quantitative differences) than they are a difference in kind (qualitative differences). Instead of dividing people into discrete categories of psychopaths and non-psychopaths, the psychopathy construct orders people along a continuum of psychopathy (Guay et al., 2007). Second, it means that psychopathy is probably the consequence of an additive etiological process in which one's position on the psychopathy continuum is a function of the number of risk factors currently active in a person's life (Farrington, 1998).

Table 1. Taxometric Studies on Psychopathy

Study	Sample	Measure	IND	Procedures	COMP	OUT
Harris et al. (1994)	653 mentally disordered offenders	PCL-R	N	C, BR, BA	N	T
Skilling et al. (2001)	1111 school-age boys	PCL:YV	N	M, C, G, BR	N	T
Marcus et al. (2004)	309 jail and prison inmates	PPI	Y	M, E, L	Y	D
Vasey et al. (2005)	386 children and adolescents	APSD	Y	M, C, E, L, BR	Y	T
Edens et al. (2006)	876 prison inmates/substance abusers	PCL-R	Y	M, E. L	Y	D
Guay et al. (2007)	4865 forensic patients/prison inmates	PCL-R	Y	M, E, L	Y	D
Harris et al. (2007)	512 sexual offenders	PCL-R	Y/N	M, C. E	N	T
Murrie et al. (2007)	757 delinquent boys	PCL:YV	Y	M, E, L	Y	D
Walters, Duncan et al. (2007)	409 prison inmates	PCL-R	Y	M, E, L	Y	D
Walters, Gray et al. (2007)	2250 forensic patients/prison inmates	PCL:SV	Y	M, E, L	Y	D
Coid and Yang (2008)	638 general population adults	PCL:SV	Y	M	N	T
Walters, Brinkley et al. (2008)	1972 prison inmates	LSRP	Y	M, E, S, L	Y	D
Edens et al. (2010)	723 delinquent youth	APSD, PPI	Y	M, C, L	Y	D
Walters et al. (2011)	503 sexual offenders	PCL-R	Y	M, C, L	Y	D

Note. Measure = assessment measure from which indicators were constructed; PCL-R = Psychopathy Checklist-Revised; PCL:YV = Psychopathy Checklist-Youth Version; PPI = Psychopathic Personality Inventory; APSD = Antisocial Process Screening Device; PCL:SV = Psychopathy Checklist-Screening Version; LSRP = Levenson Self-Report Psychopathy scale; IND = quasi-continuous indicators containing at least four ordered categories; Y = yes; N = no; Procedures = taxometric procedures; M = mean above minus below a cut (MAMBAC), C = maximum covariance (MAXCOV), E = maximum eigenvalue (MAXEIG); S = maximum slope (MAXSLOPE); L = latent-mode factor analysis (L-Mode); BR = base rate consistency; BA = Bayesian analysis; G = goodness of fit index (GFI); COMP = use of taxonic and dimensional comparison curves; OUT = outcome; T = taxonic, D = dimensional

Third, it means that instruments designed to assess psychopathy must be capable of assessing different levels of the construct, rather than placing individuals into mutually exclusive groups of psychopaths and non-psychopaths (Walters, Gray et al., 2007). Fourth, it means that instead of labeling someone a psychopath it is more appropriate to talk about a person's degree of psychopathy or position on the psychopathy continuum (Edens et al., 2006). All four implications are inconsistent with Robert Hare's view of psychopathy as a distinct type as reflected in statements he makes in the preface of his best-selling book, *Without Conscience* (Hare, 1993): "Psychopaths are social predators who charm, manipulate, and ruthlessly plow their way through life...Completely lacking in conscience and in feelings for others, they selfishly take what they want and do as they please, violating social norms and expectations without the slightest sense of guilt or regret" (p. ix). In light of a growing body of research suggesting that the latent structure of psychopathy is dimensional, sentiments, like those expressed by Hare (1993) above, may be more caricature than science.

Empirical Controversy #3: Is Antisociality a Core Feature of Psychopathy?

Robert Hare based his theory of psychopathy (Hare, 1970) and the PCL-R (Hare, 2003) on the work of psychiatrist Hervey Cleckley (1941/1988) who listed "inadequately motivated antisocial behavior" as a core feature of psychopathic personality. However, the reactive antisocial behavior and impulse crimes of the Clecklian psychopath differ widely from the proactive antisocial behavior and planned crimes that dominate current versions of the psychopathy construct. Antisocial behavior in the psychopath, according to Cleckley (1941/1988), is committed for "small stakes and under much greater risks of being discovered...[and with an] absence of any apparent goal" (p. 341) than the antisocial behavior of the non-psychopathic criminal. Cleckley's reactive view of psychopathic antisocial behavior is very different from contemporary perspectives on psychopathic antisocial behavior in which the proactive or instrumental aspects of antisociality are emphasized. Research, based largely on the PCL-R, has identified proactive or instrumental aggression and criminality as more prominent in the Harian psychopath than in non-psychopathic criminals (Cornell et al., 1996; Glenn and Raine, 2009; Porter and Woodworth, 2006). In effect, then, the antisociality found in Hare's version of the psychopathy construct, operationally defined as Facet 4 (antisocial) of the PCL-R, may not be the same antisociality that Cleckley identified as a core feature of psychopathy.

Using exploratory and confirmatory factor analysis and principles from item response theory (IRT), David Cooke and Christine Michie (2001) arrived at the controversial conclusion that antisocial behavior, as measured and conceptualized by the PCL-R, was not a core feature of psychopathy. Cooke, Michie, and Hart (2006) contend that instead of being a root cause or core component of psychopathy, antisocial behavior is actually a consequence or correlate of psychopathy. Cooke and colleagues enlist four theoretical arguments in support of their consequence hypothesis: (1) classical clinical descriptions of psychopathy (Cleckley, 1941/1988; McCord and McCord, 1964; Schneider, 1950) often do not include antisocial behavior as a primary symptom of the disorder; (2) psychopathy is more often the cause than the consequence of antisocial behavior (McDermott et al., 2000); (3) antisocial behavior consists of specific behavioral acts as opposed to the general personality traits that have traditionally defined psychopathy (Blackburn, 1988); (4) psychopathic personality traits account for only a small portion of the variance in antisocial behavior (Gottfredson and Hirschi, 1990). Cooke and Michie's (2001) analyses revealed the presence of three principal factors or dimensions of psychopathy— arrogant and deceitful interpersonal style, deficient affective experience, and impulsive and irresponsible behavioral style—none of which included a single antisocial behavior item.

Hare and his colleagues take issue with the conclusion that antisocial behavior is not part of the psychopathy construct. Hare and Neumann (2008, 2010), for instance, believe that a fourth facet (antisocial behavior) should be added to Cooke and Michie's (2001) three-factor model (interpersonal, affective, and lifestyle) to form a complete picture of how PCL-R-measured psychopathy is structured. They buttress their argument with the claim that they uncovered confirmatory factor analytic support for their four-factor model. Even some of their own data, however, to include the results of item response theory analyses reported in the PCL-R test manual (Hare, 2003) and a book chapter (Hare and Neumann, 2006), indicate that the antisocial facet is inferior to the first three facets (interpersonal, affective, lifestyle) in assessing the psychopathy construct. The controversy over the factor structure of PCL-R-measured psychopathy shows no signs of abating, with strong opinions being expressed on both sides (Hare and Neumann, 2010; Skeem and Cooke, 2010). Further study is obviously required, but the results of a recent study on two small to moderately sized samples provided further support for the three-factor model (Walters, 2012). The three-factor PCL-R hierarchical model of psychopathy is reproduced in Figure 1 and the four-factor PCL-R hierarchical model of psychopathy is reproduced in Figure 2.

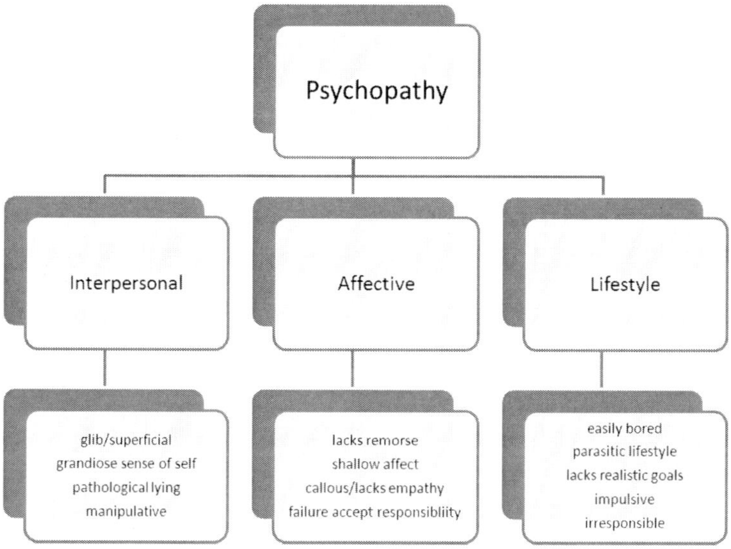

Figure 1. The Hierarchical Three-Factor Model.

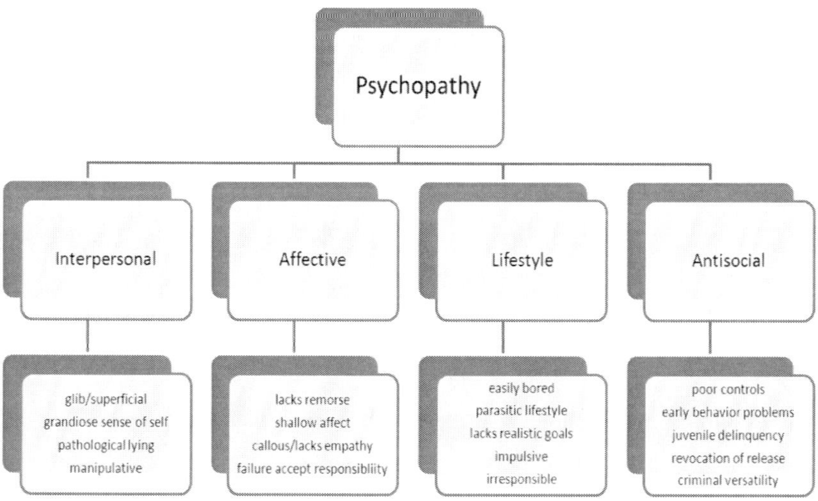

Figure 2. The Hierarchical Four-Factor Model.

EMPIRICAL CONTROVERSY #4: DOES PSYCHOPATHY PREDICT CRIMINAL JUSTICE OUTCOMES?

The foundation of the argument that psychopathy is indispensible to the criminal justice system is based on the belief that the PCL-R is "unparalleled" in predicting violent and non-violent recidivism in the community and violent and non-violent disciplinary problems in prison (Hare, 1996; Hemphill, Hare, and Wong, 1998). Whereas the PCL-R was originally designed to assess psychopathy, it has been increasingly used for risk assessment. However, the results of meta-analyses comparing the PCL-R to alternate risk assessment procedures—the Lifestyle Criminality Screening Form (LCSF: Walters, White, and Denney, 1991) and the Level of Service Inventory-Revised (LSI-R: Andrews and Bonta, 1995), for instance—denote that these less time-intensive procedures are capable of predicting criminal justice outcomes at least as well as the more time-intensive PCL-R. Walters (2003), for one, determined that the Lifestyle Criminality Screening Form and PCL-R performed comparably in predicting recidivism and institutional infractions as evidenced by overlapping effect size confidence intervals. Unfortunately, only one of the studies in the Walters (2003) meta-analysis (i.e., Kroner and Mills, 2001) covered both the Lifestyle Criminality Screening Form and PCL-R and so there is a need for more research directly comparing these two measures. In a meta-analysis of the Level of Service Inventory-Revised and PCL-R, Gendreau, Goggin, and Smith (2002) determined that the Level of Service Inventory-Revised exceeded the PCL-R in predicting general and violent recidivism, although as in the Walters (2003) meta-analysis, the effect size confidence intervals for the Level of Service Inventory-Revised and PCL-R overlapped extensively and only a handful of studies directly compared the two procedures.

Research reviewed in an earlier section of this chapter seemed to suggest that Facet 4 (antisocial) may not be a core feature of psychopathy. This just said, of the four PCL-R facets, Facet 4 is often the best predictor of criminal justice outcomes (see Table 2). It is therefore possible that the PCL-R owes much of its predictive power to Facet 4 despite the fact Facet 4 is not a core feature of psychopathy. Walters and colleagues (Walters and Heilbrun, 2010; Walters, Knight, Grann, and Dahle, 2008; Walters, Wilson, and Glover, 2011) have formally tested this hypothesis by examining the incremental validity of Facet 4 relative to the first three PCL-R facets. Entering the first three facets into the first block and Facet 4 into the second block of a hierarchical logistic or Cox regression analysis, Facet 4 continued to display a significant predictive effect, whereas Facets 1-3 failed to achieve incremental validity relative to Facet 4 when variable order was reversed (Facet 4 at Block 1 and the other three facets at Block 2). This presents a problem for those who would argue that psychopathy plays a central role in the criminal justice system. If the ability of the PCL-R to predict recidivism and institutional violence depends largely on the contributions of a facet that is not even a core feature of psychopathy, then psychopathy may not play as central a role in the criminal justice system as has traditionally been assumed.

Whereas Facets 1-3 of the PCL-R do not possess incremental validity relative to Facet 4, it is still possible that Facets 1-3 are capable of predicting criminal justice outcomes. It could be argued, for instance, that including Facets 1-3 in the same equation as Facet 4, given a moderately high degree of intercorrelation between facets, may have concealed or "washed out" a meaningful predictive effect for the psychopathy component (i.e., Facets 1-3). To test this possibility, Walters (2012) explored the incremental validity of the first three PCL-R facets relative to two non-PCL-R measures, age and criminal history. Age at time of release from prison and the violation factor score of the Lifestyle Criminality Screening Form (LCSF-V) were used as measures of age and criminal history, respectively. The LCSF-V is a better measure of criminal history than the more commonly used number of prior arrests or convictions because it is less correlated with, and thus less biased by, age. Entering age at time of release and the LCSF-V at Block 1 and a composite of the first three PCL-R facets at Block 2 of a hierarchical logistic or Cox regression analysis revealed no incremental validity effect for the psychopathy composite (Facets 1-3) in predicting general and violent recidivism in two separate samples (Walters, 2012). When these analyses were repeated using the full PCL-R (including Facet 4) as the variable in Block 2, the PCL-R failed to achieve incremental validity in three out of four instances. A construct as vital to the criminal justice system as psychopathy should be able to predict relevant criminal justice outcomes at a level above and beyond what can be achieved with simple demographic (age) and historical (criminal history) measures. With respect to the two samples included in the Walters (2012) study, PCL-R-measured psychopathy clearly failed the test.

Table 2. Receiver Operating Characteristic (ROC) Results for the Four PCL-R Facets and the Total PCL-R Score in Ten Samples

					AUC Values						
Sample	Nation	N	Sex	Outcome	BR	FU	F1	F2	F3	F4	PCL
Heilbrun et al. (1998)	U.S.	183	M	Violent Arrest	0.4	4.2	0.56	0.54	0.56	0.61	0.59
Grann et al. (1999)	Sweden	318	M	Any Conviction	0.6	3.6	0.65	0.64	0.71	0.79	0.76
				Violent Conviction	0.4	3.6	0.63	0.6	0.64	0.7	0.69
Wilson (2000)	NZ	199	M	Violent Conviction	0.3	5	0.62	0.68	0.73	0.73	0.73
Skeem and Mulvey (2001)	U.S.	490	M	Violent Act	0.2	0.4	0.66	0.69	0.67	0.78	0.76
Skeem and Mulvey (2001)	U.S.	368	F	Violent Act	0.1	0.4	0.6	0.68	0.67	0.73	0.72
Glover et al. (2002)	Canada	105	M	Any Conviction	0.6	2	0.53	0.48	0.69	0.63	0.61
				Violent Conviction	0.3	2	0.44	0.49	0.59	0.63	0.54
Kroner et al. (2005)	Canada	400	M	Any Conviction	0.4	3.5	0.59	0.61	0.66	0.68	0.67
				Violent Conviction	0.2	3.5	0.55	0.57	0.56	0.64	0.6
Walters and Duncan (2005)	U.S.	122	M	Any Arrest	0.5	5.8	0.59	0.59	0.65	0.67	0.63
				Violent Arrest	0.1	5.8	0.52	0.55	0.57	0.57	0.56

Sample	Nation	N	Sex	Outcome	AUC Values						
					BR	FU	F1	F2	F3	F4	PCL
Dahle (2006)	FRG	307	M	Any Conviction	0.7	10	0.59	0.61	0.64	0.69	0.71
				Violent Conviction	0.3	10	0.54	0.59	0.64	0.68	0.7
Knight and Thornton (2007)	U.S.	457	M	Any Charge	0.3	2	0.58	0.57	0.63	0.67	0.66
				Victim Charge	0.1	2	0.57	0.58	0.6	0.67	0.65
Weighted Mean AUC	(k = 10)						0.6	0.61	0.65	0.7	0.68
95% Confidence Interval											
Lower Limit							0.57-	0.58-	0.62-	.0.66-	0.64-
Upper Limit							0.62	0.65	0.67	0.73	0.72

Note. All figures are areas under the receiver operating characteristic (ROC) curve; multiple AUCs from the same sample averaged before being included in the weighted mean; Nation = country where study took place, U.S. = United States of America, NZ = New Zealand, FRG = Federal Republic of Germany; N = sample size; Sex = gender, M = male, F = female; Outcome = Outcome measure; BR = base rate of outcome; FU = follow-up period (in years); AUC = Area Under the (Receiver Operating) Curve; F1 = Facet 1 (Interpersonal); F2 = Facet 2 (Affective); F3 = Facet 4 (Lifestyle); F4 = Facet 4 (Antisocial); PCL-R = PCL-R total score; Weighted Mean AUC = AUC weighted by sample size; k = number of studies included in the weighted mean effect size.

EMPIRICAL CONTROVERSY #5: IS PSYCHOPATHY TREATABLE?

Theorists as diverse as Cleckley (1941), Karpman (1946), Hare (1993), and Kernberg (1998) have expressed pessimism about society's ability to treat and do much of anything to change psychopathy. Gacono et al. (1997) are particularly skeptical about our ability to intervene with those classified as psychopathic. Their overall assessment, in fact, is that there is "nothing the behavioral sciences can offer for treating those with psychopathy" (p. 119). The Penetanguishene study is often cited by proponents of the "nothing works" perspective on psychopathy treatment. In this study, treated psychopaths were as likely to recidivate generally and significantly more likely to recidivate violently than a group of untreated psychopaths. This study has been interpreted as evidence that "therapy may make [psychopaths] worse" (Hare, 1993, p. 198). Results from another study, this one conducted by the English Prison Service, led Hare and colleagues to surmise that enrolling individuals with elevated Factor 1 scores in therapy only teaches them how to get in touch with other people's feelings as a pretense to interpersonal manipulation and exploitation (Hare, Clark, Grann, and Thornton, 2000). Both programs, however, may have been inappropriate interventions for psychopathy. The program evaluated in the Penetanguishene study, for instance, was clearly not grounded in evidence-based principles. Besides being highly coercive (participants were forced to remain in treatment), the program was run principally by inmates with minimal staff input or supervision and contained such radical interventions as nude encounter groups designed to break through the psychopathic glibness and make participants more receptive to change (Rice, Harris, and Cormier, 1992). The English Prison study, on the other hand, was not only ineffective with psychopathic offenders but with non-psychopathic offenders as well (Hare et al., 2000).

Other researchers, however, have found that some forms of intervention may be helpful in altering psychopathic patterns of behavior. Utilizing data from the MacArthur Violence Risk Assessment Study, Skeem, Monahan, and Mulvey (2002) determined that psychopaths benefitted as much from treatment as non-psychopaths and that treatment-enrolled psychopaths were just as likely to be deterred from future violence as treatment-enrolled non-psychopaths. Based on these results, Skeem et al. (2002) reject the pessimistic conclusion that psychopathy is uniformly unresponsive to intervention. In a meta-analysis of 42 treatment studies, Salekin (2002) arrived at a similar conclusion. Overall, 62% of the psychopathic individuals included in the Salekin (2002) study showed some improvement relative to a 20% rate of improvement in a no-treatment control group. Figure 3 depicts the effect sizes achieved by six different therapeutic modalities in the Salekin (2002) meta-analysis. Eclectic interventions produced moderately high effect sizes, pharmacological, psychoanalytic, and cognitive-behavioral interventions produced moderate effect sizes, and therapeutic community (TC) and electroconvulsive shock therapy (ECT) interventions produced effect sizes that were indistinguishable from those generated by the no-treatment control group. Intensive individual psychotherapy (an average of four sessions per week for at least one year), combining individual and group therapy, and including family members in treatment were associated with 91%, 81%, and 75% improvement, respectively. Whereas the research literature on treatment interventions with psychopathy suffers from a number of conceptual and methodological problems (Salekin, 2002), nowhere in this literature is there any evidence to support the nihilistic view that psychopathy is essentially untreatable.

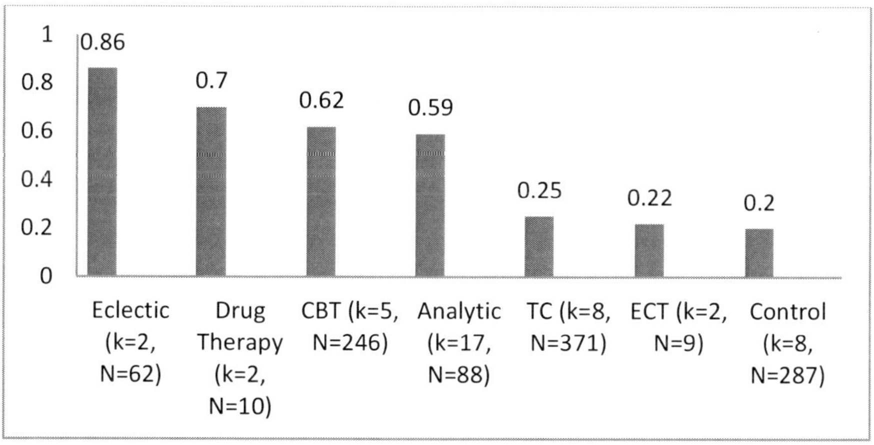

Salekin, 2002.

Note: Effect size measured as mean proportion of sample demonstrating improvement; CBT = cognitive-behavioral therapy; TC = therapeutic community; ECT = electroconvulsive therapy; k = number of studies; N = total sample size across all studies.

Figure 3. Effect Sizes for Treatment Interventions Applied to Psychopathy.

Conclusion

Gaps in knowledge are fertile soil for the development of controversies and psychopathy is no exception. With the understanding that there are significant gaps in our current understanding of psychopathy, five controversies involving psychopathy were examined in this chapter. These controversies, though far from settled, are more than simple matters of opinion. Facts relevant to each controversy need to be generated and assessed. The purpose of this chapter has been to review known facts on five controversies currently confronting psychopathy research and practice. The results of the current review suggest that extending the psychopathy construct to children and adolescents may present a number of ethical and practical problems, that psychopathy may be more accurately characterized as a dimension than a distinct category, that antisocial behavior may be a correlate rather than core feature of psychopathy, that psychopathy may not be capable of predicting criminal justice outcomes above and beyond age and criminal history, and that individuals high on the psychopathy dimension may be more responsive to treatment than has traditionally been assumed. Just because none of these controversies has been resolved does not mean that each side of the controversy is equally supported by the research literature. The data reviewed in this chapter suggest that Hare's (1970, 1993) original view of psychopathy as a developmentally based, highly stable category that is resistant to change and a highly competent predictor of criminal justice outcomes may be in error. To keep thinking along these lines in the face of a growing body of contradictory data is irrational and self-defeating. We must therefore find the courage to challenge traditional and erroneous views of psychopathy, the wisdom to generate new empirical leads, and the tenacity to thoroughly evaluate our hypotheses if we ever hope to resolve these controversies.

Note

PCL-R items are normally scored as not present (0), possibly or partially present (1), and present (2). In the Harris et al. (1994) study the PCL-R items were scored as not present (0) and present (1).

REFERENCES

Andrews, D. A., and Bonta, J. (1995). *The Level of Service Inventory—Revised.* Toronto, Canada: Multi-Health Systems.

Babiak, P., Neumann, C. S., and Hare, R. D. (2010). Corporate psychopathy: Talking the walk. *Behavioral Sciences and the Law, 28*, 174-193.

Blackburn, R. (1998). Psychopathy and personality disorder: Implications of interpersonal theory. In D. Cooke, A. Forth, and R. Hare (Eds.), *Psychopathy: Theory, research and implications for society* (pp. 269-301). Netherlands: Kluwer Academic.

Cleckley, H. (1988). *The mask of sanity* (5th ed.). St. Louis, MO: Mosby. (Original work published 1941)

Coid, J. and Yang, M. (2008). The distribution of psychopathy among a household population: categorical or dimensional? Social *Psychiatry and Psychiatric Epidemiology. 43*, 773-781.

Cooke, D. J., and Michie, C. (2001). Refining the construct of psychopathy: Towards a hierarchical model. *Psychological Assessment, 13*, 171-188.

Cooke, D. J., Michie, C., and Hart, S. D. (2006). Facets of clinical psychopathy: Toward clearer measurement. In C. J. Patrick (Ed.), *Handbook of psychopathy* (pp. 91-106). New York: Guilford.

Cornell D. G., Warren J., Hawk G., Stafford, E., Oram, G., and Pine, D. (1996). Psychopathy in instrumental and reactive violent offenders. *Journal of Consulting and Clinical Psychology, 64*, 783-790.

Dahle, K.-P. (2006). Strengths and limitations of actuarial prediction of criminal reoffense in a German prison sample: A comparative study of LSI-R, HCR-20 and PCL-R. *International Journal of Law and Psychiatry, 29*, 431-442.

Edens, J. F., Boccaccini, M. T., and Johnson, D. W. (2010). Inter-rater reliability of the PCL-R total and factor scores among psychopathic sex offenders: Are personality features more prone to disagreement than behavioral features? *Behavioral Sciences and the Law, 28*, 106-119.

Edens, J. F., Guy, L. S., and Fernandez, K. (2003). Psychopathic traits predict attitudes toward a juvenile capital murderer. *Behavioral Sciences and the Law, 21*, 807-828.

Edens, J. F., Marcus, D. K., Lilienfeld, S. O., and Poythress, N. G. (2006). Psychopathic, not psychopath: Taxometric evidence for the dimensional structure of psychopathy. *Journal of Abnormal Psychology, 115*, 131-144.

Edens, J. F., Marcus, D. K., and Vaughn, M. G. (2011). Exploring the taxometric status of psychopathy among youthful offenders: Is there a juvenile psychopath taxon? *Law and Human Behavior, 35*, 13-24.

Farrington, D. P. (1998). Predictors, causes, and correlates of youth violence. In M. Tonry and M. H. Moore (Eds.), *Youth violence* (pp. 421-475). Chicago: University of Chicago Press.

Forth, A. E., Kosson, D. S., and Hare, R. D. (2003). *Psychopathy Checklist: Youth Version (PCL:YV).* Toronto, Ontario, Canada: Multi-Health Systems.

Frick, P. J., and Hare, R. D. (2001). *The Antisocial Process Screening Device (APSD).* Toronto: Multi-Health Systems.

Frick, P. J., and Marsee, M. A. (2006). Psychopathy and developmental pathways to antisocial behavior in youth. In C. J. Patrick (Ed.), *Handbook of psychopathy* (pp. 353–375). New York: Guilford.

Gacono, C., Nieberding, R., Owen, A., Rubel, J., and Bodholdt, R. (1997). Treating conduct disorder, antisocial, and psychopathic personalities. In J. Ashford and B. Sales (Eds.), *Treating adult and juvenile offenders with special needs* (pp. 99-129). Washington, DC: American Psychological Association.

Gendreau, P., Goggin, C., and Smith, P. (2002). Is the PCL-R really the "unparalleled" measure of offender risk? *Criminal Justice and Behavior, 29*, 397-426.

Glenn, A. L., and Raine, A. (2009). Psychopathy and instrumental aggression: Evolutionary, neurobiological, and legal perspectives. *International Journal of Law and Psychiatry, 32*, 253-258.

Glover, A. J. J., Nicholson, D. E., Hemmati, T., Bernfeld, G. A., and Quinsey, V. L. (2002). A comparison of predictors of general and violent recidivism among high-risk federal offenders. *Criminal Justice and Behavior, 29*, 235-249.

Gottfredson, M. R., and Hirschi, T. (1990). *A general theory of crime.* Stanford, CA; Stanford University Press.

Grann, M., Långström, N., Tengström, A., and Kullgren, G. (1999). Psychopathy (PCL-R) predicts violent recidivism among criminal offenders with personality disorders in Sweden. *Law and Human Behavior, 23*, 205-217.

Guay, J.-P., Ruscio, J., Knight, R. A., and Hare, R. D. (2007). A taxometric analysis of the latent structure of psychopathy: Evidence for dimensionality. *Journal of Abnormal Psychology, 116*, 701-716.

Hare, R. D. (1970). *Psychopathy: Theory and research.* New York: Wiley.

Hare, R. D. (1993). *Without conscience: The disturbing world of the psychopaths among us*. New York: Guilford.

Hare, R. D. (1996). Psychopathy: A clinical construct whose time has come. *Criminal Justice and Behavior,23*, 25-54.

Hare, R. D. (1998). The Hare PCL-R: Some issues concerning its use and misuse. *Legal and Criminological Psychology, 3*, 99-119.

Hare, R. D. (2003). *The Hare Psychopathy Checklist—Revised manual* (2nd ed.). Toronto, Ontario, Canada: Multi-Health Systems.

Hare, R. D., Clark, D., Grann, M., and Thornton, D. (2000). Psychopathy and the predictive validity of the PCL-R: An international perspective. *Behavioral Sciences and the Law, 18*, 623-645.

Hare, R. D., and Neumann, C. S. (2006). The PCL-R assessment of psychopathy: Development, structural properties, and new directions. In C. J. Patrick (Ed.), *Handbook of psychopathy* (pp. 58-88). New York: Guilford.

Hare, R. D., and Neumann, C. S. (2008). Psychopathy as a clinical and empirical construct. *Annual Review of Clinical Psychology, 4*, 217-246.

Hare, R. D., and Neumann, C. S. (2010). The role of antisociality in the psychopathy construct: Comment on Skeem and Cooke. *Psychological Assessment, 22*, 446-454.

Harris, G. T., Rice, M. E., Hilton, N. Z., Lalumière, J. L., and Quinsey, V. L. (2007). Coercive and precocious sexuality as a fundamental aspect of psychopathy. *Journal of Personality Disorders,* 21, 1-27.

Harris, G. T., Rice, M. E., and Quinsey, V. L. (1994). Psychopathy as a taxon: Evidence that psychopaths are a discrete class. *Journal of Consulting and Clinical Psychology, 62*, 387-397.

Heilbrun, K., Hart, S. D., Hare, R. D., Gustafson, D., Nunez, C., and White, A. J. (1998). Inpatient and postdischarge aggression in mentally disordered offenders: The role of psychopathy. *Journal of Interpersonal Violence, 13*, 514-527.

Hemphill, J. F., Hare, R. D., and Wong, S. (1998). Psychopathy and recidivism: A review. *Legal and Criminological Psychology, 3*, 139-170.

Karpman, B. (1946). Psychopathy in the scheme of human typology. *Journal of Nervous and Mental Disease, 103*, 276-288.

Kernberg, O. (1998). The psychotherapeutic management of psychopathic, narcissistic, and paranoid transferences. In T. Millon, E. Simonsen, M. Birket-Smith, and R. D. Davis (Eds.), *Psychopathy: Antisocial, criminal, and violent behavior* (pp. 372-382). New York: Guilford.

Knight, R. A., and Thornton, D. (2007). *Evaluating and improving risk assessment schemes for sexual recidivism: A long-term follow-up of convicted sexual offenders.* Final Report, NCJ 217618, http://nij.ncjrs.gov/publications.

Kroner, D. G., and Mills, J. F. (2001). The accuracy of five risk appraisal instruments in predicting institutional misconduct and new convictions. *Criminal Justice and Behavior, 28*, 471-489.

Kroner, D. G., Mills, J. F., and Reddon, J. R. (2005). A coffee can, factor analysis, and prediction of antisocial behavior: The structure of criminal risk. *International Journal of Law and Psychiatry, 28*, 360-374.

Levenson, M. R., Kiehl, K. A., and Fitzpatrick, C. M. (1995). Assessing psychopathic attributes in a noninstitutional population. *Journal of Personality and Social Psychology, 68*, 151-158.

Lilienfeld, S. O., and Andrews, B. P. (1996). Development and preliminary validation of a self-report measure of psychopathic personality traits in noncriminal populations. *Journal of Personality Assessment, 66*, 488-524.

Lloyd, C. D., Clark, H. J., and Forth, A. E. (2010), Psychopathy, expert testimony and indeterminate sentences: Exploring the relationship between Psychopathy Checklist—Revised testimony and trial outcome in Canada. *Legal and Criminological Psychology, 15*, 323-339.

Lynam, D. R. (1997). Pursuing the psychopath: Capturing the fledgling psychopath in a nomological net. *Journal of Abnormal Psychology, 106*, 425-438.

Lynam, D. R. (1998). Early identification or the fledgling psychopath: Locating the psychopathic child in the current nomenclature. *Journal of Abnormal Psychology, 107*, 566-575.

Marcus, D. K., John, S. L., and Edens, J. F. (2004). A taxometric analysis of psychopathic personality. *Journal of Abnormal Psychology, 113*, 626-635.

McCord, W., and McCord, J. (1964). *The psychopath: An essay on the criminal mind.* New York: Van Nostrand-Reinhold.

McDermott, P. A., Alterman, A. I., Cacciola, J. S., Rutherford, M. J., Newman, J. P., and Mulholland, E. M. (2000). Generality of Psychopathy Checklist—Revised factors over prisoners and substance-dependent patients. *Journal of Consulting and Clinical Psychology, 68*, 181-186.

Meehl, P. E. (1995). Bootstraps taxometrics: Solving the classification problem in psychopathology. *American Psychologist, 50*, 266-275.

Meehl, P. E. (2004). What's in a taxon? *Journal of Abnormal Psychology, 113*, 39-43.

Murrie, D. C., Boccaccini, M., Turner, D., Meeks, M., Woods, C., and Tussy, C. (2009). Rater (dis)agreement on risk assessment measures in sexually violent predator proceedings: Evidence of adversarial allegiance in forensic evaluation? *Psychology, Public Policy, and Law, 15*, 19-53.

Murrie, D. C., Marcus, D. K., Douglas, K. S., Lee, Z., Salekin, R. T., and Vincent, G. (2007). Youth with psychopathic features are not a discrete class: A taxometric analysis. *Journal of Child Psychology and Psychiatry,* 48, 714-723.

Olver, M. E., and Stockdale, K. C. (2010). Psychopathy and youth violence: Research, controversies and clinical utility. *British Journal of Forensic Practice, 12*(2), 3-13.

Porter S., and Woodworth M. (2006). Psychopathy and aggression. In C. J. Patrick (Ed.), *Handbook of psychopathy* (pp. 481-494). New York: Guilford.

Rice, M., Harris, G., and Cormier, C. (1992). An evaluation of a maximum security therapeutic community for psychopaths and other mentally disordered offenders. *Law and Human Behavior, 16*, 399-412.

Richards, H. (2011, May 26). Identifying the bad apples. *Expert Panel: Weighing the Value of a Test for Psychopaths.* Retrieved 7/02/11 from http://www.gpb.org/news/2011/05/26/.

Ruscio, J., Haslam, N., and Ruscio, A. M. (2006). *Introduction to the taxometric method: A practical guide.* Mahwah, NJ: Lawrence Erlbaum.

Salekin, R. T. (2002). Psychopathology and therapeutic pessimism: Clinical lore or clinical reality? *Clinical Psychology Review, 22*, 79-112.

Salekin, R. T., Rogers, R., and Sewell, K. W. (1996). A review and meta-analysis of the Psychopathy Checklist and Psychopathy Checklist-Revised: Predictive validity of dangerousness. *Clinical Psychology: Science and Practice, 3*, 202-215.

Schneider, K. (1950). *Psychopathic personalities.* London: Cassell.

Seagrave, D., and Grisso, T. (2002). Adolescent development and the measurement of juvenile psychopathology. *Law and Human Behavior, 26*, 219-236.

Skeem, J. L., and Cauffman, E. (2003). Views of the downward extension: Comparing the youth version of the Psychopathy Checklist with the Youth Psychopathic traits Inventory. *Behavioral Sciences and the Law, 21*, 737-770.

Skeem, J. L., and Cooke, D. J. (2010). Is criminal behavior a central component of psychopathy? Conceptual directions for resolving the debate. *Psychological Assessment, 22*, 433-445.

Skeem, J. L., Monahan, J., and Mulvey, E. P. (2002). Psychopathy, treatment involvement, and subsequent violence among civil psychiatric patients. *Law and Human Behavior, 26*, 577-603.

Skeem, J. L., and Mulvey, E. P. (2001). Psychopathy and community violence among civil psychiatric patients: Results from the MacArthur Violence Risk Assessment study. *Journal of Consulting and Clinical Psychology, 69*, 358-374.

Skilling, T. A., Quinsey, V. L., and Craig, W. M. (2001). Evidence of a taxon underlying serious antisocial behavior in boys. *Criminal Justice and Behavior, 28*, 450-470.

Vasey, M. W., Kotov, R., Frick, P. J., and Loney, B. R. (2005). The latent structure of psychopathy in youth: A taxometric investigation. *Journal of Abnormal Child Psychology, 33*, 411-429.

Walters, G. D. (2003). Predicting criminal justice outcomes with the Psychopathy Checklist and Lifestyle Criminality Screening Form: A meta-analytic comparison. *Behavior Sciences and the Law, 21*, 89-102.

Walters, G. D. (2004). The trouble with psychopathy as a general theory of crime. *International Journal of Offender Therapy and Comparative Criminology, 48*, 133-148.

Walters, G. D. (2012). Psychopathy and crime: Testing the incremental validity of PCL-R-measured psychopathy as a predictor of general and violent recidivism. *Law and Human Behavior, 36*, 404-412.Walters, G. D., Brinkley, C. A., Magaletta, P. R., and Diamond, P. M. (2008). Taxometric analysis of the Levenson Self-Report Psychopathy scale. *Journal of Personality Assessment, 90*, 491-498.

Walters, G. D., and Duncan, S. A. (2005). Use of the PCL-R and PAI to predict release outcome in inmates undergoing forensic evaluation. *Journal of Forensic Psychiatry and Psychology, 16*, 459-476.

Walters, G. D., Duncan, S. A., and Mitchell-Perez, K. (2007). The latent structure of psychopathy: A taxometric investigation of the Psychopathy Checklist-Revised in a heterogeneous sample of male prison inmates. *Assessment, 14*, 270-278.

Walters, G. D., Gray, N.S., Jackson, R. L., Sewell, K. W., Rogers, R., Taylor, J., and Snowden, R. J. (2007). A taxometric analysis of the Psychopathy Checklist: Screening Version (PCL:SV): Further evidence of dimensionality. *Psychological Assessment, 19*, 330-339.

Walters, G. D., and Heilbrun, K. (2010). Violence risk assessment and Facet 4 of the Psychopathy Checklist: Predicting institutional and community aggression in two forensic samples. *Assessment, 17*, 259-268.

Walters, G. D., Knight, R. A., Grann, M., and Dahle, K.-P. (2008). Incremental validity of the Psychopathy Checklist facet scores: Predicting release outcome in six samples. *Journal of Abnormal Psychology, 117*, 396-405.

Walters, G. D., Marcus, D. K., Edens, J. F., Knight, R. A., and Sanford, G. M. (2011). In search of the psychopathic sexuality taxon: Indicator size does matter. *Behavioral Sciences and the Law, 29*, 23-39.

Walters, G. D., and Ruscio, J. (2009). To sum or not to sum: Taxometric analysis with ordered categorical assessment items. *Psychological Assessment, 21*, 99-111.

Walters, G. D., White, T. W., and Denney, D. (1991). The Lifestyle Criminality Screening Form: Preliminary data. *Criminal Justice and Behavior, 18*, 406-418.

Walters, G. D., Wilson, N., and Glover, A. J. J. (2011). Predicting recidivism with the Psychopathy Checklist: Are factor score composites really necessary? *Psychological Assessment, 23*, 552-557

Wilson, N. (2000, November). *Does the PCL-SV predict serious violent reoffending for offenders appearing before the National Parole Board?* (Tech. Rep.). Hamilton, New Zealand: Corrections Psychological Service.

In: Born Bad? Critiques of Psychopathy
Editor: James Horley ISBN: 978-1-62618-082-6

Chapter 4

CLINICAL LIMITATIONS WITH THE USE OF PSYCHOPATHY

Ian V. McPhail*

Law and Mental Health Program, Centre for Addiction and Mental Health
Toronto, Ontario, Canada

INTRODUCTION

Contemporary commentators have argued for the importance of psychopathy in understanding the psychology of the forensic client and preventing future violence and aggression (Hare, 1996; Hare and Neumann, 2009; Salekin, Worley, and Grimes, 2010). There are, however, a series of questions regarding the empirical evidence and theoretical base of psychopathy (Skeem, Polaschek, Patrick, and Lilienfeld, 2011) and critiques regarding the value of psychopathy in understanding criminal behaviour (e.g., Andrews and Bonta, 2010; Walters, 2004). One of the aims of this chapter is to review evidence that suggests limits to the usefulness of psychopathy to the forensic clinician when conducting assessments of risk for future violence and identifying treatment targets. The second aim of this chapter is to understand the potential harm assessing psychopathy causes to the therapeutic relationship and the impact a diagnosis of psychopathy has on clients. These latter considerations will be based on elaborating the stigmatizing effects of

* Email: Ian.McPhail@camh.ca

psychopathy. Throughout the chapter, I will draw on my experience as a forensic clinician providing therapeutic services and conducting risk assessments with incarcerated offenders and forensic psychiatric inpatients. This discussion will hopefully provide some novel understanding of the harm the label "psychopath" has on individuals.

WHAT'S THE EVIDENCE? PSYCHOPATHY AS A PREDICTOR OF RECIDIVISM

One of the main functions of forensic clinicians is assessing risk for future violence. Risk assessment informs decisions regarding sentencing, treatment, and releasing clients to the community. Hare (1996) argues that a main reason psychopathy is vitally important to the criminal justice system is its strong relationship with future offending in forensic populations. This conclusion, on the surface, appeared to be supported by the empirical evidence at the time. Given recent research findings, the question "does psychopathy predict recidivism?" needs to be revisited.

Most of the research reviewed uses the Psychopathy Checklist-Revised (PCL-R; Hare, 2003), which is a 20 item interview and file-review based tool that assesses constructs thought to be central to psychopathy (Hare and Neumann, 2010). The items of the PCL-R are generally found to load onto 2 underlying dimensions; Factor 1 includes items that assess affective and interpersonal characteristics (e.g., superficially charming, pathological lying, and a grandiose sense of self-worth) and Factor 2 captures general antisocial behaviour and criminality (e.g., criminal versatility, juvenile delinquency; Hare, 2003). While other measures of psychopathy exist, the vast majority of research conducted to date focuses on the PCL-R, which is considered by some to be the "gold standard" in assessing the construct of psychopathy (Fulero, 1995) and is used widely throughout the criminal justice system (McGrath, Cumming, Burchard, Zeoli, and Ellerby, 2009).

Recent meta-analytic research has raised questions regarding the accuracy of certain conclusions (e.g.,, Hare, 1996; Salekin, Rogers, and Sewell, 1996) regarding the value of psychopathy in predicting recidivism. A meta-analysis is a type of research method that includes a systematic review of an area of research literature that is germane to a specific research question. Researchers will use statistical techniques to combine the findings of multiple research studies and attempt to provide a quantitative average of the results from the group of studies. Singh, Grann, and Fazel (2011) conducted a meta-analysis comparing the accuracy of nine different assessment tools in predicting violent re-offending. Singh and colleagues report that the PCL-R had significantly lower predictive validity than the Sexual Violence Risk-20 (Boer, Hart, Kropp, and Webster, 1997), Sex Offender Risk Appraisal Guide (Quinsey, Harris, Rice, and Cormier, 2006), and Violence Risk Appraisal Guide (Quinsey et al., 2006) in predicting violent re-offence and was ranked as the least accurate out of the nine risk assessment tools. When the assessment tools were rank ordered in terms of performance across four outcome statistics, the PCL-R was ranked eighth, with three of the instruments ranked higher developed mainly for the prediction of sexual re-offending, not violent re-offending. Other meta-analytic reviews have reached similar conclusions (Edens, Campbell, and Weir, 2007; Walters, 2003a, 2003b; Yang, Wong, and Coid, 2010). These meta-analytic findings challenge the view that the PCL-R is an unparalleled measure of forecasting future re-offending (Salekin et al., 1996).

Meta-analytic research findings appear to support the following conclusions regarding the validity of psychopathy for predicting future violence by forensic clients. First, other risk assessment measures are superior at predicting outcomes of interest to the forensic clinician. Second, the affective characteristics thought to be central to the construct of psychopathy are weakly associated with violent and unrelated to sexual recidivism (Walters, 2003). Third, considering the affective characteristics of psychopathy does not add incremental predictive utility beyond considering historical anti-social behaviour (Skeem and Mulvey, 2001; Walters, Knight, Grann, and Dahle, 2008) and other risk assessment tools (Looman, Morphett, and Abracen, 2012). Forth, most of the 20 items of the PCL-R are unrelated to violent and sexual re-offending (Coid, Yang, Ullrich, Zhang, Sizmur, Farrington, and Rogers, 2011; Langevin and Curnoe, 2011). To summarize, the affective and interpersonal characteristics thought to be the central features of "psychopaths", such as their ability to charm and manipulate anyone for personal gain, that they are adept liars who derive pleasure from misleading others, or their inability to experience remorse or guilt for abusing or taking advantage of others have generally been found to be unrelated to future violence. These research findings provide serious doubt regarding the usefulness of assessing for psychopathy in forensic contexts.

WHERE'S THE VALUE? PSYCHOPATHY AS A CRIMINOGENIC NEED

Over the past 20 years, forensic psychology has produced evidence that support the conclusion that some treatment programs reduce recidivism in a variety forensic populations, especially if treatment follows general guiding principles (Abracen, Looman, Ferguson, Harkins, and Mailloux, 2010; Andrews and Bonta, 2010; Hanson, Bourgon, Helmus, and Hodgson, 2009; Lipsey, 1995; Poleschek, 2010, 2011). Andrews and Bonta (2010) suggest that forensic interventions should provide more intensive treatment for clients at higher risk to re-offend (Risk principle). To most effectively reduce re-offending, interventions should focus on criminogenic needs, which are risk factors demonstrated to be related to re-offending and that are theoretically changeable through intervention (Need principle). In the previous section, research relevant to the Risk principle was reviewed and psychopathy was suggested to be of little value compared to other risk assessment tools in predicting violent and sexual re-offending, and by extension, identifying higher risk clients. In the current section, I will critique the value of psychopathy as a criminogenic need for the forensic clinician.

The assumption that "psychopathy predicts recidivism" is hazardous due to the downward extension that the affective and interpersonal characteristics of measures of psychopathy are predictive of re-offending. These characteristics might be construed as changeable and amenable to treatment, and as a result, are appropriate treatment targets for interventions aimed to reduce re-offending. The empirical evidence suggests that these affective and interpersonal characteristics of psychopathy are generally unrelated to violent (Coid et al., 2011) and sexual re-offending (Langevin and Curnoe, 2011). Given these findings, I would suggest that the affective characteristics of psychopathy, as measured by the PCL-R, are not criminogenic needs. Further, the assessment of psychopathy in order to identify treatment targets in forensic interventions aimed at reducing recidivism is not warranted.

When assessing for risk-relevant treatment targets in forensic settings, there are other psychological constructs more salient a client's risk to re-offend. Specifically, with clients with sexual offence histories, it is important to address issues such as substance abuse and deviant sexual interests in treatment programs (Abracen, Looman, and Langton, 2008). The value of such constructs lays in the strong empirical relationship with sexual recidivism, the important place these constructs have in theory on sexual offending, and that these constructs can be targeted in treatment. Further, there is evidence that substance abuse predicts violent recidivism after psychopathy is statistically controlled for (Hildebrand, de Ruiter, and Vogel, 2004) and that lifetime alcohol use makes an incremental contribution to sexual recidivism prediction after controlling for risk for recidivism and psychopathy in sex offenders (Looman and Abracen, 2011). Other constructs, such as sociosexuality, or a willingness to engage in frequent and casual sexual encounters, may effectively diminish the relationship between psychopathy and sexual aggression perpetration (Mouilsa and Calhoun, 2012). These and other constructs have also been found to co-occur or cluster in therapeutically meaningful ways (Hermann, McPhail, Helmus, and Hanson, 2012; Mandeville-Norden and Beech, 2009; McPhail, Hermann, Fernandez, and Isa, 2012; Seto and Fernandez, 2011) and are included in current risk assessment instruments that measure treatment needs for forensic clients (Hanson, Harris, Scott, and Helmus, 2007; Thornton, 2002). For example, emotional congruence with children, which is marked by a desire to spend time with children, considering children to be friends, and emotionally identifying with children predicts sexual interests in prepubescent children and cognitions supportive of sex with children (McPhail et al., 2012; Hermann et al., 2012). These results make an individual client's risk for re-offence clear: the desire to be around children and have them as friends, being sexually aroused by children, and having cognitions that sex with children is acceptable provide clear indications of what targets may be fruitful when working with clients therapeutically. When compared with psychological constructs that have a robust empirical, theoretical, and importantly, clinical value in understanding and treating sexual offenders, psychopathy does not appear to have much room to improve our understanding. In addition, current theoretical models of understanding sexual recidivism spend little time considering the value of psychopathy in clarifying why sexual offenders re-offend (Mann, Hanson, and Thornton, 2010; Thakker and Ward, 2011).

Conclusions on Risk and Need Considerations

One important psychological theory of criminal behaviour indicates that high risk, high need clients are readily identifiable by forensic clinicians and "that there is *no need to hypothesize* the construct of psychopathy" to aid this process (Andrews and Bonta, 2010, pp. 218, italics added). I have offered the view that assessing for psychopathy will not contribute to understanding a client's risk for re-offending or identifying treatment needs and thus provides little information to be used in case conceptualization or risk management. Andrews and Bonta (2010) phrased this position succinctly, "What is the added value of having a construct such as psychopathy or APD [Anti-social Personality Disorder]? With respect to the prediction of criminal behaviour, we suspect none" (2010, pp. 221). Empirical evidence seems to support this claim, especially as it relates to sexual violence.

There are a number of treatment needs that are more important in helping clients deal with the problems that are relevant to desisting from crime. In reference to sexual offenders, Abracen et al. (2008) argued that key targets in treatment with sexual offenders include substance abuse issues and deviant sexual interests (see also Abracen and Looman, 2006; Looman and Abracen, 2011). These types of psychological constructs, that are highlighted by Hanson and Morton-Bourgon (2005) and elaborated by McPhail, Hermann, and Nunes (2012) and Helmus, Hanson, Babchishin, and Mann (2013), are relevant to the clinical outcomes that forensic clinicians are generally concerned with. To summarize, there is little reason for a forensic clinician to assess a client for psychopathy in order to more fully understand risk for re-offence and the presenting treatment needs that should be addressed in treatment. As Walters (2003b) highlights, there needs to be a clear value for undertaking the assessment of psychopathy that takes a minimum of 3-4 hours (in my experience, the time require is usually double this amount) in order for a clinician to justify his or her use of limited resources. Psychopathy does not present as a justifiable assessment and treatment target given the current state of knowledge.

WHAT'S THE HARM? PSYCHODIAGNOSIS AS DETRIMENT TO CHANGE AND THE INDIVIDUAL

Thus far in the chapter, I have been concerned with how psychopathy might be used to inform decisions regarding specific outcomes in forensic contexts and have put forward strong conclusions regarding the limits of psychopathy's usefulness. From here, the focus changes to considerations of the *harm* associated with the use of psychopathy on the therapeutic process and the individual client. The consideration of therapeutic processes and those factors that promote or interfere with positive therapeutic process is important, in part, because these processes will ultimately affect treatment participation and progress and further, recidivism. While considerations of the potential harm to clients may be considered from the perspective of the clinician [i.e., in terms of engaging a client and a client's readiness and motivation to make changes], it might be valuable to further explore the harm to the client outside of the therapeutic relationship to more fully understand the damaging effects of this psychodiagnosis.

Psychological Assessment as Therapeutic

For forensic clinicians engaged in psychotherapy with forensic clients, the assessment of psychopathy may have a deleterious effect on the therapeutic relationship and outcomes. An emerging consideration in the general clinical psychology and counselling literature concerns the effects psychological assessment and providing assessment feedback has on clients and therapeutic outcomes (Finn and Tonsanger, 2002). Preliminary meta-analytic research points to the positive impact using psychological assessment as a therapeutic intervention has on both process (e.g., working alliance, hope, session depth) and outcome variables (e.g., premature treatment termination, days hospitalized, symptomatology; Poston and Hanson, 2010). For psychological assessment to have a positive therapeutic effect, it necessarily needs to be collaborative, provide meaningful and agreed upon directions in therapy, and forge an empathetic connection to clients (Poston and Hanson, 2010). While forensic assessment places limits on client input in some instances, these themes in assessment as therapeutic intervention seem consistent with general rehabilitative efforts in forensic psychology (Marshall, Marshall, Serran, and O'Brien, 2011; Ward and Maruna, 2007). For example, Ward and Maruna (2007) argue that creating and maintaining a therapeutic alliance is essential to motivating change. A positive therapeutic alliance includes a collaborative spirit and having the client feel that a clinician respects them. The process of creating an empathetic connection to a client or using diagnostic constructs to subsume aspects of a client's idiosyncratic experience of the world (Kelly, 1955) appears to be inherently at odds with a clinician labelling a client as a psychopath.

This is the case for multiple reasons. First, a client has very little room to shine a positive light on such a label, as the general public's conception of "psychopaths" is negative and pejorative (Horley, 2011). Second, a client would not readily agree that the diagnosis of "psychopath" has the ability to accurately and pervasively describe his or her identity and experience. In my experience, I have discussed this label with diagnosed clients as they try to make sense of the label and what it means for them. For some, they dismiss the label outright and call the clinician an "asshole". Others take the label seriously and try to figure out what it means and how they came to acquire the label. One went so far as to purchase Hare's book on psychopathy, *Without Conscience* (1993) and read it while in segregation. The book brought little clarification, especially on the point of "Well, if I'm a psychopath, then I'm a psychopath. What do I do to stop being one?" Unfortunately, I had little to offer in response. Third, the use of "psychopathy" as a diagnostic construct does little to inspire optimism for change for the client. The potential for optimism for the future is essential for a diagnostic construct to be of clinical value (Kelly, 1955) and is vital for the clinician to create in a therapeutic relationship to be successful with forensic clients (Fernandez and Mann, 2010). Lastly, as was argued in the first sections, there appears to be little value for assessing psychopathy in terms of providing a direction for treatment. Whatever gain may be argued for assessing psychopathy is heavily outweighed by the potential consequences within the therapeutic relationship and to the outcomes that rely on the creation of a positive therapeutic alliance.

Beyond the potential damage to the rehabilitative efforts of a forensic clinician, there might always be the sense that "psychopaths" truly are those individuals who deserve the harshest forms of social control because they possess some of the worst characteristics one might possess. We are then justified in placing this stigmatizing and shameful label on the individual in order to mitigate the damage they may cause (Arneson, 2007). This account suggest considering the "moral value" of using psychopathy against the hazards because any tool available to us cannot be cast aside without considering its value to a society (Arneson, 2007). However, high-risk, high-need clients do show appropriate treatment gains and that these offenders of the highest risk are successfully managed in the community (Wilson, Cortoni, and McWhinnie, 2009) at costs much lower than indefinite incarceration (Elliott and Beech, 2012). At a functional level, psychopathy may not work as well as other labels, like "high-risk, high-need" client at guiding treatment to ameliorate those intrapersonal psychological dispositions that prevent clients from becoming acculturated into the larger prosocial culture. Instead, there are two current theories of crime and rehabilitation (Risk-Need-Responsivity model, Andrews and Bonta, 2010; Good Lives Model, Laws and Ward, 2011; Ward, 2002; Ward and Maruna, 2007) that guide the generation of clinical hypotheses to reduce and manage risk and promote those events and life processes that encourage desistance (Maruna, 2001). If, as a function of the requirements of the work forensic clinicians do, the process of labelling is inevitable, this process should be based on those theoretical constructions of the crime-desistance process that allow for the most clear and plausible explications of how a client might "make good" (Maruna, 2001). Given these damaging effects, psychopathy belongs in the waste basket due in part to the minimal value it appears to offer when compared to other psychological constructs and the potential damaging effects that the label has on rehabilitative efforts.

THE STIGMA OF PSYCHOPATHY

Stigma refers to a set of stereotypic beliefs about an attribute or characteristic of an individual (Jones, Farina, Hastorf, Markus, Miller, and Scott, 1984), the process that links an attribute of an individual to undesirable characteristics (Goffman, 1963), and discrimination imposed upon and experienced by an individual due to the stigmatizing attribute (Link and Phelan, 2001). Link and Phelan (2001) argue that stigma includes the construction of labels and the linkage of these labels with stereotyped beliefs and discrimination. Psychopathy exists as a category defined in the empirical and theoretical psychology and psychiatric literature, but is also linked to stereotypic beliefs by some of those same literatures (e.g.,, Cleckley's [1976] *The Mask of Sanity* or Hare's [1993] *Without Conscience: The Disturbing World of Psychopaths among Us*). Horley (2011) argues that the pejorative nature of psychopathy is well understood by the general public and these meanings are readily elicited by many of us, including those who receive the label. To a general audience, psychopathy is inexorably connected to individuals like Theodore Bundy, John Wayne Gacy Jr., Paul Bernardo, Jeffrey Dahmer, or pulp fiction crime villains (e.g., the Joker from Batman comics; Moore, 1988). There are ready-made and readily accessible constructions of the "psychopath" on television shows that detail fictional stories of "sadistic, psychopathic" sexual killers or *CNN* news reports on the destructive behaviour of business executives. These sources act to communicate the stereotypic beliefs associated with the label "psychopath" to the general public, giving the beginnings for a "lay theory of psychopathy" (Link and Phelan, 2001).

Lay theories are key components to the creation and maintenance of stigma (Link and Phelan, 2001). These are negative or undesirable characteristics associated with a label we learn in childhood and adolescence and retain in our adulthood. This is why we are able to connect the label "psychopath" with an entire set of undesirable characteristics, or stereotypic beliefs, without much effort. A lay theory is important mainly because it imparts the reasons why a stigmatized person is justifiably excluded, cast aside, and treated as a dangerous or unknown "other". A lay theory of psychopathy has multiple sources, however, it may be of value to narrow down the number of sources in order to construct a set of characteristics that psychopathy is connected to by the general public[1]. Table 1 presents a list of characteristics one would expect the label "psychopath" to elicit. Due to a lay theory of psychopathy, members of society know why they do not like, are afraid of, and punish those who bear the label "psychopath".

Lay theories also inform the "psychopath" why they are being stigmatized and excluded and may be a source of self-stigma. So-called psychopaths will have knowledge of the cultural stereotypes that are collectively associated with the label. If the labelled individual assesses the stereotypes as legitimate, they may accept this negative view to the detriment of their own psychological well-being via self-stereotyping (Yang, Kleinman, Link, Phelan, Lee, and Good, 2007). This is the way stigma "gets under the skin" and produces a host of negative psychological outcomes in stigmatized populations (Hatzenbuehler, 2009, p. 707). One "psychopath" I worked with was aware of what the label meant and shared that he thought it made him a completely rotten person if this was the type of person he is. This process of learning and reinforcing stereotypes is a foundational component to adopting a self-stigma and can also block an individual's attempts to rejoin the norm (Scheff, 1966). Lay theories of psychopathy and labelling go beyond promoting discrimination against "psychopaths" to also encouraging the "psychopath" to accept the bad press about who clinicians and the general public or media say they are. Horley (2011) points out that a label like psychopathy becomes self-fulfilling and may impede rehabilitative efforts by forensic clinicians by prompting clients to lose hope for the possibility of change.

[1] It is important to note from the start, this endeavour is not to make culprits out of these commentators and administer blame for the intentional or unintentional creation of cultural stereotypes, rather the endeavour is to find some fundamental components of a lay theory of psychopathy.

Table 1. Attributes of Psychopaths in a Lay Theory of Psychopathy

Source	Attribute
Cleckley (1976)	• Absence of nervousness or anxiety in the face of danger • Incapable of loving others • Inability to learn from past failures • Pursues impersonal sex with multiple, concurrent partners • No life plan
Hare (1993)	• Smooth talking conman • Excessive lying; exceptionally convincing • "Remain absolutely unflappable even after [the] deceit [is] revealed." (p. 14) • "Can play a concerto on anyone's heartstrings" (p. 207) • Emotionless predators • Able to trap anyone in a web that will ultimately be harmful • Know how to spot potential victims • Nothing works to make them stop their destructive behaviour; psychopaths see no need to change or revise their behaviour • See very little wrong with themselves and that their destructive behaviour is rational and enjoyable • Believe manipulation and deceit are legitimate • "Always getting into trouble" (p. 194)
Wikipedia entry for "Psychopathy"	• False emotions • Selfish • Grandiose • Aggressive • Dangerous/evil • Born criminals • Missing basic human qualities that promote social cohesion • Amoral • Instrumentally violent • Cold-blooded
Wikipedia entry for "Fictional Portrayals of Psychopaths"	• Ideal villains • Highly skilled at killing people • Disarming charisma

Lay theories also inform the "psychopath" why they are being stigmatized and excluded and may be a source of self-stigma. So-called psychopaths will have knowledge of the cultural stereotypes that are collectively associated with the label. If the labelled individual assesses the stereotypes as legitimate, they may accept this negative view to the detriment of their own psychological well-being via self-stereotyping (Yang, Kleinman, Link, Phelan, Lee, and Good, 2007). This is the way stigma "gets under the skin" and produces a host of negative psychological outcomes in stigmatized populations (Hatzenbuehler, 2009, p. 707). One "psychopath" I worked with was aware of what the label meant and shared that he thought it made him a completely rotten person if this was the type of person he is. This process of learning and reinforcing stereotypes is a foundational component to adopting a self-stigma and can also block an individual's attempts to rejoin the norm (Scheff, 1966). Lay theories of psychopathy and labelling go beyond promoting discrimination against "psychopaths" to also encouraging the "psychopath" to accept the bad press about who clinicians and the general public or media say they are. Horley (2011) points out that a label like psychopathy becomes self-fulfilling and may impede rehabilitative efforts by forensic clinicians by prompting clients to lose hope for the possibility of change.

THE STIGMA OF PSYCHOPATHY IN THE CRIMINAL JUSTICE SYSTEM

The foregoing discussion of a lay theory of psychopathy provides some context regarding the undesirable characteristics ascribed to "psychopaths" and why certain negative outcomes may be imposed upon individuals who receive this label. This includes negative outcomes like structural discrimination (i.e., court rulings; clinicians ascribing low treatment amenability scores to psychopaths or disallowing psychopaths from participating in treatment) and individual discrimination (i.e., decisions made by parole officers regarding transferring a client to lower security institutions) imposed upon labelled psychopaths by the criminal justice system (CJS). This section will discuss some of the empirical literature on the topic of psychopathy and discrimination to increase our understanding of what outcomes are influenced by the stigma of psychopathy.

In Canada, psychopathy is used by forensic clinicians in settings such as dangerous offender hearings. A dangerous offender hearing involves a judge making a decision whether an individual, who has previously been found guilty of a violent offence, meets the criteria of posing a significant threat of harm to others and thus deserves a preventative indeterminate sentence. In a study that reviewed expert testimony in dangerous offender hearings, psychopathy was found to have a significant relationship with how an expert rated an offender's treatment amenability, with the more psychopathic individuals being rated as less amenable to treatment (Lloyd, Clark, and Forth, 2010). In turn, ratings of treatment amenability were strongly related to the outcome of the hearing, with lower ratings of treatment amenability being associated with a higher likelihood of sentencing an offender to an indeterminate sentence. This research supports Foucault's (1995; see also Federman, Holmes, and Jacob, 2009) argument that stigma (i.e., "psychopaths are not amenable to treatment") is a mechanism used to legitimize the use of social control. In the example of the courtroom, society is justified in handing down an indeterminate sentence because an offender is unlikely to benefit from treatment and be successfully managed in the community because he is a "psychopath". These outcomes are examples of structural discrimination associated with the label "psychopath".

Recent research has examined other negative outcomes associated with the stigma of psychopathy. Expert reports of psychopathic personality traits tend to exert negative influence on judges' recommendations regarding intensive community supervision for young offenders and the view of a youth as dangerous and likely to continue offending into adulthood (Murrie, Boccaccini, McCoy, and Cornell, 2007). These findings were also reported in a sample of probation officers (Murrie, Cornell, and McCoy, 2005). In addition, forensic clinicians rated youth described as having psychopathic traits as higher risk, however, did not view these youths as less likely to benefit from treatment (Rockett, Murrie, and Boccaccini, 2007). It is interesting to note that the use of the diagnostic label "psychopathy" did not have a strong effect on negative outcomes in the above studies. However, use of the more colloquial phrase "is a psychopath" was found to have a strong effect on the belief of potential jurors in juvenile cases that the youth posed a higher risk for re-offence and was deserving of harsher punishment (Boccacini, Murrie, Clark, and Cornell, 2008). This belief in harsher punishment for "psychopaths" might not extend to jurors decisions in capital murder trials (Cox, DeMatteo, and Foster, 2010). However, the use of this label may have more subtle deleterious effects, such as leading jurors to disregard mitigating factors in mock capital murder cases (Edens, Guy, and Fernandez, 2003). As Lloyd and colleagues (2010) indicate, the mix of empirical results does not provide clear advice for a clinician to minimize potential labelling effects in CJS contexts, as it seems in some instances a label of “psychopath” will have a deleterious effect on decision-makers, while in others, describing an offender using psychopathic trait descriptions will produce negative labelling effects. The empirical literature provides some evidence of the effect the stigma of psychopathy has in producing structural inequalities for individuals who receive this label.

The influence of the stigma of psychopathy in the criminal justice system might more rightly be called structural discrimination (Link and Phelan, 2001; Sayce, 1998). Structural discrimination takes place when an institution (i.e., the CJS) creates and enforces policies that are intended to reduce the opportunities of a labelled group (Corrigan, Markowitz, and Watson, 2004). Recent research using psychopathy in CJS contexts provides some examples of the structural discrimination associated with the forensic clinician’s use of the label “psychopath”. The term ‘discriminationd is not used here to provoke sympathy for these cases. What is intended is to identify the actors who supply the stigmatizing label (forensic clinicians) and the various exclusionary outcomes that this label produces, to locate psychopathy within processes of structural discrimination, and promote further consideration by forensic clinicians of the consequences associated with the label. This review hopefully will encourage forensic clinicians to thoroughly consider the stigmatizing effects that are created by this construct.

Self-Stigma and the Individual Offender

To more fully consider the stigma of psychopathy, the impact of this psychodiagnosis on the internal world of the affected forensic client should be considered. Most of the literature regarding psychopathy and stigmatizing effects has focused on the structural component of stigma. Little, if any, research has been conducted with samples of “psychopaths” and the experiences of being labelled as such. Due to this, the discussion will focus on work regarding self-stigma with other stigmatized populations, such as gay/lesbian groups, those diagnosed with severe mental illness, sexual offenders, or those with HIV/AIDS. The fundamental element of these discussions of self-stigma is that diagnostic labelling has deleterious psychological effects on the affected individuals and these effects cause additional difficulties for the individuals, exacerbating the original difficulties linked to stigma-related exclusion (Link, Cullen, Stuening, Shrout, and

Dohrewend, 1989). Considering elements of self-stigma in so-called psychopaths is required to more fully understand how this label operates in the forensic-clinical setting.

Self-stigma, or internalized stigma, involves processes whereby an individual is aware of and endorses negative stereotypes about a certain group, perceives these stereotypes to be self-relevant, incorporates these negative evaluations into their own self, and anticipates social rejection or status loss due to their stigma (Corrigan, Kerr, and Knudsen, 2005; Goffman, 1963; Link et al., 1989; Livingston and Boyd, 2010). When an individual begins to accept a stigma and incorporate negative evaluations based on the stigma into her understanding of herself, this process is characterized by negative feelings about self, maladaptive behaviour, and can impeded recovery or compound suffering (Livingston and Boyd, 2010). As displayed in Table 1, a lay theory of psychopathy is readily available and it is likely those who receive the label "psychopath" are aware of the negative characteristics others will view them as having. As well, in my clinical experience, offenders have been aware of the potential discrimination that they face if bearing this mark. This awareness of the stigma and discrimination associated with the stigma of psychopathy suggests that these offenders' experience follows the experiences expected from modified labelling theory in sociology (Link et al., 1989). In addition, this awareness opens the possibility for self-stigma and other negative effects for so-called psychopaths.

Current psychological models of stigma also link negative psychological outcomes to stigma-related stress, which are stressors an individual or group face due to the stigma associated with a label (Hatzenbuehler, 2009). These stressors may relate to the fear of being discovered or withdrawal from opportunities due to anticipated discrimination (Link et al., 1989; Mingus and Birchfield, 2012). Stigma-related stress is thought to cause coping and emotional regulation problems, social problems, and cognitive processing problems that all elevate the risk for psychopathology. In forensic populations, theory and research indicate that psychological deficits such as emotional dysregulation or cognitive processing problems will contribute to the potential for future criminal activity and aggression (Andrews and Bonta, 2010; Baumeister and Lobbestael, 2011; McMurran, 2011; Novaco, 2011). In the case of the "psychopath", fear of discovery/exposure or facing longer prison sentences prompted by their own awareness of the effects of this label may exacerbate pre-existing risk factors for violence and aggression. While this is not directly self-stigma, this model of stigma-related stress indicates the psychological processes that are affected by the individual's awareness and experience of stigma and discrimination.

Another consideration is the experience of shame by stigmatized individuals. In my experience, shame was frequently brought up in discussion by so-called psychopathic offenders. The experience of shame appeared to come from multiple labelling sources: "psychopath", "criminal"[2], and being an inmate at the particular institution I was working within. For one offender, his awareness of the stigma was most acute when he was in crowded public places. This was related to a number of perceptions of himself, but was also due to the awareness that others will identify that he is a criminal and a psychopath. To him, the idea of these critical eyes on him was a source of anxiety, a long-standing history of avoidance of social situations, and self-destructive behaviour such as substance abuse. These perceptions and experiences of the "mark of stigma" fit in with Goffman's classic doctrine on stigma (1963) and Hatzenbeuhler's (2009) psychological mediation framework of stigma. This offender experienced increased stress and hypervigilance due to the stigma he carried and his fear of discovery. Indeed, this offender took measures to conceal the marks that would give him away to the general public (e.g., covering up tattoos) and engaged in social withdrawal and avoidance. I would offer that if not exposed to psychological tools with which to manage the experience of anxiety, hypervigilance, and shame, there may be negative psychological consequences for stigmatized clients. Seen in this way, labels and stigma might be catalysts for future substance use and aggressive behaviour for clients who have substance abuse and violent histories.

The experience of shame is not a new experience to most "psychopathic" clients, as research generally shows marked childhood trauma, neglect, and victimization for these offenders (Daversa, 2010; Graham, Kimonis, Wasserman, and Kline, 2012; Marshall and Cooke, 1999). For "psychopathic" clients I have worked with, their childhoods were steeped in neglect and abuse; as they grew older, adolescent and adult substance abuse, marginalization, and numerous incarcerations were common experiences. For some, receiving the label of psychopath did not serve to taint his sense of basic

[2] Indeed, there are very real economic penalties applied to those who carry the "criminal" stigma in the form of lower wages from employers (Funk, 2004; Rasmusen, 1996) or unemployment (Furuya, 2002). This aspect of stigma may actually increase the chance of re-offence (Funk, 2004). There seems to be a general criminal stigma with real social consequences awaiting "psychopathic offenders" upon their release from prison that is in addition to effects experienced while incarcerated (e.g.,, removal from treatment opportunities).

moral worth because this label came when he was 40 or 50 years old and stigma and shame was experienced long before a forensic clinician applied the label. The psychopathic label served not to introduce shame, but rather to push the shame deeper and give it a new facet upon which the client could reflect upon the fundamental unfairness of life and his own despicable nature[3]. Evidence of the true badness of his nature had pervaded his experience from an early age; the label "psychopath" was further proof and a further burden to carry. In addition to potentially damaging outcomes caused by the label of psychopathy, Horley (2011) suggests that such labels are re-affirming, as the label "explains" the damage caused by the individual and he willing accepts the label as it confirms his behaviour was caused by the immutable badness of his nature. Seen in this light, a label of psychopathy becomes a positive for the individual. But it is also a negative experience because the danger remains that he will then act out the violent, harmful social role of the "psychopath". In discussing self-stigma and psychopathy, I would argue that shame, perceptions of the badness of the self, and anxiety are all relevant in understanding the experience of affected individuals.

What I found amazing about these clients was the effort to maintain hope in their abilities, the future, and the therapeutic relationship; if resilience exists, these individuals were interesting manifestations of it. However, this hope and resilience was certainly threatened by the diagnostic label, "psychopath" (indeed, hope is negatively affected in other stigmatized groups; Livingston and Boyd, 2010), mostly due to the individual client's awareness of the negative and undesirable characteristics that the label elicits. As a clinician, I believe counteracting these processes requires encouraging hope and providing opportunities to build self-esteem and a sense of empowerment. However, current research supports the conclusion that internalized stigma has a deleterious effect on these processes and treatment adherence (Livingston and Boyd, 2010). Given that the specific population that forensic clinicians are engaged with may have had a long standing history of shame and personal failures, it appears counterproductive to take actions that likely contribute to diminishing the chances of encouraging important processes, like hope and self-esteem. Indeed, some argue that encouraging these processes is the basis of therapeutic work with forensic populations (Marshall et al., 2011).

[3] Some commentators maintain that labels applied to individuals through the action of the state (i.e., institutional actors of the state, such as courts, or individual actors on behalf of the state, forensic experts) have especially powerful stigmatizing effects (Goffman, 1963). However, there is some evidence that multiple labels do not produce a cumulative stigmatizing effect (Livingston, Rossiter, Verdun-Jones, 2011).

SUMMARY AND CONCLUSION

The foregoing sections on the utility of psychopathy in assessing risk for re-offending and identifying treatment targets suggest that measures of psychopathy have limited value, especially when compared to other methods of assessing risk for future violence and other psychological constructs to address in treatment. These are critical considerations in the work conducted by forensic clinicians. The current state of knowledge suggests that assessing psychopathy has little additional value for forensic clinicians. The use of psychopathy may even have a detrimental effect on the treatment efforts of clinicians, which also suggests that psychopathy assessment has no place in the toolbox of the clinician. Other factors outside of traditional psychological concerns were also discussed in the context of the harm caused by the the "psychopath" label. I outlined a set of characteristics that likely constitute a lay theory of psychopathy that is readily accessible to the general public. A lay theory gives life to the pejorative characteristics that promote and justify stigma and discrimination against socalled psychopaths. Research on this topic is needed to further elaborate and identify the content of a lay theory of psychopathy and what potential discrimination against "psychopaths" individuals in society are willing to support. The few studies that have examined structural discrimination directed toward "psychopaths" have produced novel results. Together these studies suggest that there are consequences for the client in criminal justice settings due to a finding of psychopathy. Further research into the applications and consequences of psychopathy in the field are needed to more fully understand the stigma and negative outcomes associated with psychopathy. A lay theory also provides another interesting insight into the stigma of psychopathy: it allows for us to see the labelled individual as having access to what the larger society thinks of them, which, in sociological theory, provides the material for self-stigma and its associated negative effects. Ultimately, the use of the psychopathic label fails to capture the complexity of forensic clients and forces us away from considering the sometimes traumatic histories of the client and understanding he or she as, in some instances, victims themselves. I would argue that this occurs at our own detriment, as clinicians are inevitably less successful in rehabilitative efforts which inevitably leads to a higher chance of future victims. The detrimental effects on the client are also important, as they do not receive the services they may need to improve their psychological wellbeing, the labeling process may produce additional psychological suffering for these clients and may prompt discriminatory practices to be used against them. The limited value of psychopathy to inform the routine work of forensic clinicians and its potential to harm the client suggests that the construct be put back on the shelf.

References

Abracen, J., and Looman, J. (2006). Evaluation of Civil Commitment criteria in a high-risk sample of sexual offenders. *Journal of Sexual Offender Civil Commitment: Science and the Law, 1*, 124-140.

Abracen, J., Looman, L., Ferguson, M., Harkins, L., and Mailloux, D. (2010). Recidivism among treated sexual offenders and comparison subjects: Recent outcome data from the Regional Treatment Centre (Ontario) high-intensity Sex Offender Treatment Programme. *Journal of Sexual Aggression, 17,* 142-152. doi: 10.1080/13552600903511980

Abracen, J., Looman, J., and Langton, C. M. (2008). Treatment of sexual offenders with psychopathic traits: Recent research developments and clinical implications. *Trauma, Violence, and Abuse, 9,* 144-166. doi: 10.1177/1524838008319633

Andrews, D. A., and Bonta, J. (2010). *The psychology of criminal conduct* (5th ed.). New Providence, New Jersey: Anderson Publishing.

Arneson, R. J. (2007). Shame, stigma, and disgust in the decent society. *The Journal of Ethics, 11,* 31-63. doi: 10.1007/s10892-006-9007-y

Baumeister, R. F., and Lobbestael, J. (2011). Emotions and antisocial behaviour. *Journal of Forensic Psychiatry and Psychology, 22,* 635-649. doi: 10.1080/14789949.2011.617535

Boccaccini, M. T., Murrie, D. C., Clark, J. W., and Cornell, D. G. (2008). Describing, diagnosing, and naming psychopathy: How do youth psychopathy labels influence jurors? *Behavioral Sciences and the Law, 26,* 487-510. doi: 10.1002/bsl.821

Boer, D. P., Hart, S. D., Kropp, P. R., and Webster, C. D. (1997). *Manual for the Sexual Violence Risk–20: Professional guidelines for assessing risk of sexual violence.* Burnaby, BC: Simon Fraser University, Mental Health, Law, and Policy Institute.

Cleckley, H. (1976). *The mask of sanity* (4th ed.). Saint Louis: C. V. Mosby Company.

Coid, J. W., Yang, M., Ullrich, S., Zhang, T., Sizmur, S., Farrington, D., and Rogers, R. (2011). Most items in structured risk assessment instruments do not predict violence. *Journal of Forensic Psychiatry and Psychology, 22,* 3-21. doi: 10.1080/14789949.2010.495990

Corrigan, P., Kerr, A., and Knudsen, L. (2005). The stigma of mental illness: Explanatory models and methods for change. *Applied and Preventive Psychology, 11,* 179-190.

Corrigan, P. W., Markowitz, F. E., and Watson, A. C. (2004). Structural levels of mental illness stigma and discrimination. *Schizophrenia Bulletin, 30,* 481–491.

Cox, J., DeMetteo, D. S., and Foster, E. E. (2010). The effect of Psychopathy Checklist-Revised in capital cases: Mock jurors' responses to the label of psychopathy. *Behavioral Sciences and the Law, 28,* 878-891. doi: 10.1002/bsl.958

Daversa, M. T. (2010). Early environmental predictors of the affective and interpersonal construct of psychopathy. *International Journal of Offender Therapy and Comparative Criminology, 54,* 6-21. doi: 10.1177/0306624X08328754

Edens, J. F., Campbell, J. S., and Weir, J. M. (2007). Youth psychopathy and criminal recidivism: A meta-analysis of the Psychopathy Checklist measures. *Law and Human Behavior, 31,* 53–75. doi:10.1007/s10979-006-9019-y

Edens, J. F., Guy, L. S., and Fernandez, K. (2003). Psychopathic traits predict attitudes toward a juvenile capital murderer. *Behavioral Sciences and the Law, 21,* 807–828.

Elliott, I. A., and Beech, A. R. (2012). A U.K. cost-benefit analysis of Circles of Support and Accountability intervention. *Sexual Abuse: A Journal of Research and Treatment.* Advanced online publication. doi: 10.1177/1079063212443385

Federman, C. Holmes, D., and Jacob, J. D. (2009). Deconstructing the psychopath: A critical discursive analysis. *Cultural Critique, 72,* 36-65.

Fernandez, Y. M., and Mann, R. E. (2009). Sexual deviations. In J. Thomas and M. Hersen (eds.), *Handbook of Clinical Psychology Competencies* (pp. 957-982). Springer Science.

Finn, S. E., and Tonsager, M. E. (2002). How Therapeutic Assessment became humanistic. *The Humanistic Psychologist, 30,* 10-22

Foucault, M. (1995). *Discipline and punish: The birth of the prison.* New York: Random House.

Fulero, S. (1995). Review of the Hare Psychopathy Checklist-Revised. In J. C. Conoley, J. C. Impara, and L. L. Murphy (Eds.), *Twelfth mental measurements yearbook* (pp. 453-454). Lincoln, NE: Buros Institute.

Funk, P. (2004). On the effective use of stigma as a crime-deterrent. *European Economic Review, 48,* 715-728. doi: 10.1016/j.euroecorev.2003.11.003

Furuya, K., 2002. A socio-economic model of stigma and related social problems. *Journal of Economic Behavior and Organization 48,* 281–290.

Goffman, E. (1963). *Stigma: Notes on the management of spoiled identity.* Englewood Cliffs, New Jersey: Prentice-Hall.

Graham, N., Kimonis, E. R., Wasserman, A. L., and Kline, S. M. (2012). Associations among childhood abuse and psychopathy facets in male sexual offenders. *Personality Disorders: Theory, Research, and Treatment, 3,* 66-75. doi: 10.1037/a0025605

Hanson, R. K., Bourgon, G., Helmus, L., and Hodgson, S. (2009). *A meta-analysis of the effectiveness of treatment for sexual offenders: Risk, need, and responsivity* (Research Report No. 2009-01). Ottawa, Ontario, Canada: Corrections Research, Public Safety Canada.

Hanson, R. K., Harris, A. J. R., Scott, T. L., and Helmus, L. (2007). *Assessing the risk of sexual offenders on community supervision: The dynamic supervision project* (Research report 2007-05). Ottawa, Ontario: Public Safety Canada.

Hanson, R. K., and Morton-Bourgon, K. E. (2005). The characteristics of persistent sexual offenders: A meta-analysis of recidivism studies. *Journal of Consulting and Clinical Psychology, 73*, 1154–1163. doi:10.1037/0022-006X.73.6.1154

Hare, R. D. (1993). *Without conscience: The disturbing world of the psychopaths among us.* New York: The Guilford Press.

Hare, R. D. (1996). Psychopathy: A clinical construct whose time has come. *Criminal Justice and Behaviour, 23,* 25-54.

Hare, R. D. (2003). *The Hare Psychopathy Checklist-Revised* (2nd ed.). Toronto, Ontario, Canada: Multi-Health Systems.

Hare, R. D., and Neumann, C. S. (2009). Psychopathy: Assessment and forensic implications. *The Canadian Journal of Psychiatry, 54,* 791-802.

Hare, R. D., and Neumann, C. S. (2010). The role of antisociality in the Psychopathy Checklist: Comment on Skeem and Cooke (2010). *Psychological Assessment, 2,* 446-454. doi: 10.1037/a0013635

Hatzenbuehler, M. L. (2009). How does sexual minority stigma "Get under the skin"? A psychological mediation framework. *Psychological Bulletin, 135,* 707-730. doi: 10.1037/a0016441

Helmus, L., Hanson, R. K., Babchishin, K. M., and Mann, R. E. (2013). Attitudes supportive of sexual offending predict recidivism: A meta-analysis. *Trauma, Violence, and Abuse, 14,* 34-53. doi: 10.1177/1524838012462244

Hermann, C. A., McPhail, I. V., Helmus, L., and Hanson, R. K. (Submitted for publication). *Correlates of emotional congruence with children in sexual offenders against children: A replication and expanded test of theoretical models with a large community sample.*

Hildebrand, M., de Ruiter, C., and Nijman, N. (2004). PCL-R psychopathy predicts disruptive behavior among male offenders in a Dutch forensic psychiatric hospital. *Journal of Interpersonal Violence, 19*, 13–29. doi:10.1177/0886260503259047

Horley, J. (2011). On the tyranny of professional labelling. *Psychotherapy and Politics International, 9,* 127-133. doi: 10.1002/ppi.244

Jones, E., Farina, A., Hastorf, A., Markus, H., Miller, D. T., and Scott, R. (1984). *Social stigma: The psychology of marked relationships.* New York: Freeman.

Kelly, G. A. (1955). *The psychology of personal constructs* (Vol 1). New York: Norton.

Langevin, R., and Curnoe, S. (2011). Psychopathy, ADHD, and brain dysfunction as predictors of lifetime recidivism among sex offenders. *International Journal of Offender Therapy and Comparative Criminology, 55,* 5-26. doi: 10.1177/0306624X09360968

Laws, D. R., and Ward, T. (2011). *Desistance from sex offending: Alternatives to throwing away the keys.* New York: Guilford Press.

Link ,B. G., Cullen, F. T., Struening, E., Shrout, P., Dohrenwend, B. P. (1989). A modified labelling theory approach in the area of mental disorders: An empirical assessment. *American Sociological Review, 54,* 100–123.

Link, B. G., and Phelan, J. C. (2001). Conceptualizing stigma. *Annual Review of Sociology, 27,* 363-385.

Lipsey, M. W. (1995). "What do we learn from 400 research studies on the effectiveness of treatment of juvenile delinquency?" In J. McGuire (ed.), *What works: Reducing reoffending, Guidelines for research to practice* (pp. 63-78). West Sussex, UK: John Wiley and Sons.

Livingston, J. D., and Boyd, J. E. (2010). Correlates and consequences of internalized stigma for people living with mental illness: A systematic review and meta-analysis. *Social Science and Medicine, 71,* 2150-2161. doi: 10.1016/j.socscimed.2010.09.030

Livingston, J. D., Rossiter, K. R., Verdun-Jones, S. N. (2011). 'Forensic' labelling: An empirical assessment of its effects on self-stigma for people with severe mental illness. *Psychiatry Research, 188,* 115-122. doi: 10.1016/j.psychres.2011.01.018

Lloyd, C. D., Clark, H. J., and Forth, A. E. (2010). Psychopathy, expert testimony, and indeterminate sentences: Exploring the relationship between Psychopathy Checklist-Revised testimony and trial outcome in Canada. *Legal and Criminological Psychology, 15,* 323-339. doi: 10.1348/135532509X468432

Looman, J., and Abracen, J. (2011). Substance abuse among high-risk sex offenders: Do measures of lifetime history of substance abuse add to the prediction over actuarial risk assessment instruments? *Journal of Interpersonal Violence, 26,* 683-700. doi: 10.1177/0886260510365871

Looman, J., Morphett, N. A. C., and Abracen, J. (2012). Does consideration of psychopathy and sexual deviance add to the predictive validity of the Static-99R? *International Journal of Offender Therapy and Comparative Criminology,* advanced online publication. doi: 10.1177/0306624X12444839

Mandeville-Norden, R., and Beech, A. R. (2009). Development of a psychometric typology of child molesters: Implications for treatment. *Journal of Interpersonal Violence, 24,* 307-324. doi: 10.1177/0886260508316479

Mann, R.E., Hanson, R.K., and Thornton, D. (2010). Assessing risk for sexual recidivism: Some proposals on the nature of psychologically meaningful risk factors. *Sexual Abuse: A Journal of Research and Treatment, 22,* 191-217. doi: 10.1177/1079063210366039

Marshall, L. A., and Cooke, D. J. (1999). The childhood experiences of psychopaths: A retrospective study of familial and societal factors. *Journal of Personality Disorders, 13,* 211-225.

Marshall, W. L., Marshall, L. E., Serran, G. A., and O'Brien, M. D. (2011). *The rehabilitation of sexual offenders: Strengths-based approach.* Washington, DC: American Psychological Association.

Maruna, S. (2001). *Making good: How ex-convicts reform and rebuild their lives.* Washington D.C.: American Psychological Association.

McGrath, R. J., Cumming, G. F., Burchard, B. L., Zeoli, S., and Ellerby, L. (2009). Current practices and emerging trends in sexual abuser management: The Safer Society 2009 North American survey. Brandon, Vermont: Safer Society Press.

McMurran, M. (2011). Emotions and antisocial behaviour: An introduction to the special issue. *Journal of Forensic Psychiatry and Psychology, 22,* 629-634. doi: 10.1080/14789949.2011.617533

McPhail, I. V., Hermann, C. A., Fernandez, Y. M., and Isai, E. (Submitted for publication). *Correlates of emotional congruence with children in sexual offenders against children: Part 1. A test of theoretical models with an incarcerated sample.*

McPhail, I. V., Hermann, C. A., and Nunes, K. L. (Submitted for publication). *Emotional congruence with children: A meta-analytic review.*

Mingus, W., and Burchfield, K. B. (2012). From prison to integration: Applying modified labeling theory to sex offenders. *Criminal Justice Studies: A Critical Journal of Crime, Law and Society, 25,* 97-109. doi: 10.1080/1478601X.2012.657906

Moore, A. (1988). *The killing joke.* New York: DC Comics.

Mouilso, E. R., and Calhoun, K. S. (2012). A mediation model of the role of sociosexuality in the associations between narcissism, psychopathy, and sexual aggression. *Psychology of Violence, 2,* 16-27. doi: 10.1037/a0026217

Murrie, D. C., Boccaccini, M. T., McCoy, W. K., and Cornell, D. G. (2007). Diagnostic labeling in juvenile court: How do descriptions of psychopathy and conduct disorder influence judges? *Journal of Clinical Child and Adolescent Psychology, 36,* 228-241. doi: 10.1080/15374410701279602

Murrie, D. C., Cornell, D. G., and McCoy, W. K. (2005). Psychopathy, conduct disorder, and stigma: Does diagnostic labeling influence juvenile probation officers recommendations? *Law and Human Behavior, 29,* 323-342. doi: 10.1007/s10979-005-2415-x

Novaco, R. W. (2011). Anger dysregulation: Driver of violent offending. *Journal of Forensic Psychiatry and Psychology, 22,* 650-668. doi: 10.1080/14789949.2011.617536

Polaschek, D. L. L. (2010). Treatment non-completion in high-risk violent offenders: Looking beyond criminal risk and criminogenic needs. *Psychology, Crime, and Law, 16,* 525-540. doi: 10.1080/10683160902971048

Polaschek, D. L. L. (2011). High-intensity rehabilitation for violent offenders in New Zealand: Reconviction outcomes for high- and medium-risk prisoners. *Journal of Interpersonal Violence, 26,* 664-682. doi: 10.1177/0886260510365854

Poston, J. M., and Hanson, W. E. (2010). Meta-analysis of psychological assessment as a therapeutic intervention. *Psychological Assessment, 22,* 203-212. doi: 10.1037/a0018679

Quinsey, V.L., Harris, G.T., Rice, M.E., and Cormier, C.A. (2006). *Violent offenders: Appraising and managing risk* (Second Edition). Washington, DC: American Psychological Association.

Rasmusen, E. (1996). Stigma and self-fulling expectations of criminality. *Journal of Law and Economics, 39,* 519–543.

Rockett, J. L., Murrie, D. C., and Boccaccini, M. T. (2007). Diagnostic labeling in juvenile justice settings: Do psychopathy and conduct disorder findings influence clinicians? *Psychological Services, 4,* 107-122. doi: 10.1037/1541-1559.4.2.107

Salekin, R., Rogers, R., and Sewell, K. (1996). A review and meta-analysis of the Psychopathy Checklist and Psychopathy Checklist-Revised: Predictive validity of dangerousness. *Clinical Psychology: Science and Practice, 3,* 203–215. doi:10.1111/j.1468-2850.1996.tb00071.x

Salekin, R. T., Worley, C., and Grimes, R. D. (2010). Treatment of psychopathy: A review and brief introduction to the mental model approach for psychopathy. *Behavioral Sciences and the Law, 28,* 235-266. doi: 10.1002/bsl.928

Sayce, L. (1998). Stigma, discrimination and social exclusion: What's in a word? *Journal of Mental Health,* 7, 331–343.

Scheff, T. J. (1966). *Being mentally ill: A sociological theory*. Chicago, IL: Aldine de Gruyter.

Seto, M. C., and Fernandez, Y. M. (2011). Dynamic risk groups among adult male sexual offenders. *Sexual Abuse: A Journal of Research and Treatment, 23,* 494-507. doi: 10.1177/1079063211403162

Singh, J. P., Grann, M., and Fazel, S. (2011). A comparative study of violence risk assessment tools: A systematic review and metaregression analysis of 68 studies involving 25,980 participants. *Clinical Psychology Review, 31,* 499-513. doi: 10.1016/j.cpr.2010.11.009

Skeem, J. L., and Mulvey, E. P. (2001). Psychopathy and community violence among civil psychiatric patients: Results from the MacArthur Violence Risk Assessment study. *Journal of Consulting and Clinical Psychology, 69,* 358–374. doi:10.1037/0022-006X.69.3.358

Skeem, J. L., Polaschek, D. L. L., Patrick, C. J., and Lilienfeld, S. O. (2011). Psychopathic personality: Bridging the gap between scientific evidence and public policy. *Psychological Science in the Public Interest, 12,* 95-162. doi: 10.1177/1529100611426706

Thakker, J., and Ward, T. (2011). An integrated theory of sexual reoffending. *Psychiatry, Psychology, and Law,* online publication. doi: 10.1080/13218719.2011.561765

Thornton, D. (2002). Constructing and testing a framework for dynamic risk assessment. *Sexual Abuse: A Journal of Research and Treatment, 14,* 139-153. doi: 10.1023/A:1014620214905

Walters, G. (2003a). Predicting institutional adjustment and recidivism with the Psychopathy Checklist factor scores: A meta-analysis. *Law and Human Behavior, 27,* 541-558.

Walters, G. D. (2003b). Predicting criminal justice outcomes with the Psychopathy Checklist and Lifestyle Criminality Screening Form: A meta-analytic comparison. *Behavioral Sciences and the Law, 21,* 89–102. doi:10.1002/bsl.519

Walters, G. D. (2004). The trouble with psychopathy as a general theory of crime. *International Journal of Offender Therapy and Comparative Criminology, 48,* 133-148. DOI: 10.1177/0306624X03259472

Walters, G. D., Knight, R. A., Grann, M., and Dahle, K. P. (2008). Incremental validity of Psychopathy Checklist facet scores: Predicting prelease outcome in six samples. *Journal of Abnormal Psychology, 117,* 396-405. doi: 10.1037/0021-843X.117.2.396

Ward, T. (2002). The management of risk and the design of good lives. Australian Psychologist, 37, 172-179.

Ward, T., and Maruna, S. (2007). *Rehabilitation.* London: Routledge.

Wikipedia entry on "Psychopathy". Accessed on February 14th, 2012.

Wikipedia entry on "Fictional portrayals of psychopaths". Accessed on February 14th, 2012.

Wilson, R. J., Cortoni, F., and McWhinnie, A. J. (2009). Circles of support and accountability: A Canadian national replication of outcome findings. *Sexual Abuse: A Journal of Research and Treatment, 21,* 412-430. doi: 10.1177/1079063209347724

Yang, L. H., Kleinman, A., Link, B. G., Phelan, J. C., Lee, S., and Good, B. (2007). Culture and stigma: Adding moral experience to stigma theory. *Social Science and Medicine, 64,* 1524-1535. doi: 10.1016/j.socscimed.2006.11.013

Yang, M., Wong, S. C. P., and Coid, J. (2010). The efficacy of violence prediction: A meta-analytic comparison of nine risk assessment tools. *Psychological Bulletin, 136,* 740-767. doi: 10.1037/a002047

In: Born Bad? Critiques of Psychopathy
Editor: James Horley
ISBN: 978-1-62618-082-6

Chapter 5

Born Bad? Labels, Morals, and Alternatives to Psychopathy

James Horley*

University of Alberta, Camrose, Alberta, Canada

Introduction

While the introduction of psychopathy and its variants into the professional and public lexicon of the mid-20th century was well received in certain circles, it created numerous difficulties. Many of these difficulties have been of a methodological nature, a few have been more theoretical, and many more have concerned clinical issues. Some of these specific issues have been examined in the previous chapters in this volume.

Rather than review more particular points here, I will consider two overarching issues that I believe are essential in any critique of psychopathy. First, the impact of labeling is an important concern for some of us in the human sciences; second, while morality tends to be avoided, it appears germane to the topic of psychopathy. A discussion of some implications of, and remedies for, these difficulties will follow.

* Email: jhorley@ualberta.ca

PROBLEMS WITH LABELS

The terms that we employ to describe ourselves and others appear to matter profoundly, and some of the most powerful labels are those employed by professionals who, with the weight of authority such as science, produce and wield the sorts of terms that appear to defy denial. However well intentioned, the labels used by mental health professionals in the course of psychodiagnosis, labels such as psychopath, do have powerful consequences. Hare (1993) and others who use psychopathy regularly claim to be concerned with the consequences of their labeling, but their concerns are often focused on 'accurate' labels rather than the use of psychodiagnoses more broadly. Thankfully, some clinicians concerned with the consequences of pronouncing individuals psychopathic or not do consider the broader implications of the labeling process-- Edens and Petrila (2003), for example, have expressed concerns about the impact of a psychopathy diagnosis on children and juveniles—but, as I have argued previously (Horley, 2011), we should be concerned with the broader issues surrounding the psychodiagnostic process on all recipients of labels like psychopath.

Social scientists have described and documented labeling effects from various perspectives. Becker (1963) presented a social response theory of deviance, where the social labeling of an anomalous/non-normative specific behavior or course of action can permit an individual to be described as deviant. Becker's focus was on minor deviants such as marijuana smokers but Sarbin (1967), following a similar line of thinking, argued that those individuals who behave in very strange, chronic manners are likely to be described as 'crazy' or 'mentally ill'. For Sarbin, this does not mean that craziness or mental illness exists except insofar as some people are placed into such a category and treated differently, often stigmatized and discriminated against. Indeed, Szasz has argued for years that use of various terms under the heading 'mental illness' is nothing more than an attempt by authorities to ostracize those plagued by problems in living (e.g., see Szasz, 1974). Scheff, too, saw the imposition of a sick role on those seen as psychiatrically disabled through various social means, including court decisions and psychiatric ward placement (Scheff, 1964), as key to subsequent psychological symptoms. More recently, a number of researchers and psychotherapists have argued along similar lines, although frequently from rather different theoretical positions, against the use of terms like mental illness or related labels (e.g., Raskin and Epting, 1993).

The impact of a more limited set of labels, the psychodiagnostic terms of the *Diagnostic and Statistical Manual (DSM*; APA, 2000), has been considered by a variety of writers. Caplan (1995) has condemned the entire effort of the American Psychiatric Association (APA) since the first appearance of the manual (APA, 1952). She cites, among other problems, the rather limited perspective of the *DSM* organizing committee that leads to certain groups (e.g., women, the poor) being over-pathologized. Verhaeghe (2004), too, has criticized the direction of the *DSM* in terms of pursuing only observable symptoms. For Verhaeghe, the approach of the APA promotes conformity in patients through negative labeling of the expressions of their underlying psychological disturbances, and no linkages to therapies are provided by the approach, and there is some evidence that *DSM* labeling has a negative impact on psychotherapeutic process (Honos-Webb and Leitner, 2001).

The extremely pejorative meanings of psychopathy and related terms like anti-social personality disorder (APD) are well known to the general public through popular writings, including the work of forensic psychologists (e.g., Hare, 1993) intended for public consumption. Forensic clients who are diagnosed as psychopathic or APD appear to me to be well aware of the negative aspects of such terms. From my interviews with thousands of clients, the most common views of their so-called psychopathic characteristics include "born bad", "damaged", "dangerous", "rotten bastard", "emotionless", "pathological liar", "don't care for others", and "completely fucked up". Generally, they see their prospects as bleak because "there's no cure" in part due to "it's in the genes". Some, to be sure, are not so grim in their personal assessment, and they seem to embrace the label of psychopath, at least insofar as they knew that there was something different or "wrong" with them and such a diagnosis confirmed their suspicions. It also allowed them to pursue their lives of murder and mayhem because "this is who I am, I can't change". Much of my effort in psychotherapy with such an individual involves challenging such a notion or, at the very least, that it describes the client in any meaningful manner. My first question is often "So what does psychopath mean to you?" and the answer is often a quizzical look or a return question such as "Don't you know?" or perhaps "You're the shrink, right? You tell me!" The quandary that I face, and other therapists who attempt to defeat the impact of such labels must deal with as well, is that it is the mental health professions which provide these labels, this self-knowledge. We must argue against ourselves, our own colleagues, to say in effect that they need to forget what respected professionals have told them, perhaps over years. It appears that such labels or self-constructions (Kelly, 1955)—information about the self which is very powerful and reassuring, hence positive (see Horley, 2008)—can become self-fulfilling for many individuals. Many resist with good reason my attempts, no doubt construed as daft by many clients, to claim that they are not truly what they have been told they are. After all, they can argue, the diagnosis is confirmed by their life of crime and/or causing pain to all those around them for many years, despite my attempts to suggest that the terms are only applied after considering their personal criminal and anti-social histories. Very few of my clients come into therapy with me questioning their psychodiagnoses, but the ones who do wonder, however timidly and tentatively, are often the individuals who I see turn their lives around, not only for a few weeks or months but over the long-term. Their rejection of limiting and negative self-definition allows them to construct a more successful self-identity, one that is not doomed by the constraints of such notions as psychopath.

Given the possible, harsh personal consequences of such labels as psychopath or APD, why would any clinician employ such terminology? I would not accuse any of my colleagues of being deliberately nasty or sadistic, although some forensic clinicians no doubt are less than effective therapeutically from years of working with less than ideal clients in working conditions that can only generously be described as less than ideal. There are likely many reasons for the use of harmful labels. Unquestionably some forensic mental health workers believe in psychiatric nosologies like the *DSM*, despite the lack of precision and reliability that almost all established systems demonstrate, because they believe in a variety of perceived benefits. Parsimony is one perceived benefit—busy clinicians overloaded with overwhelming caseloads need to be able to assess clients quickly and impart the results briefly. With unclear meanings associated with many diagnoses like APD and psychopathy, however, this benefit seems more illusory than real. Many of us deal regularly with dangerous individuals who deceive and who appear to lack any remorse or concern for their victims, but can we expect a single label to convey precisely how dangerous we truly feel they are and in what manner? How much of a sentence do we feel a judge or jury should impose on a convicted felon? By the time the details of any assessment are spelled out for a court, an agency, or another clinician, the addition of a diagnostic label is likely unnecessary unless another purpose is to be addressed.

Unfortunately, a label like psychopath appears to serve a number of other purposes. For some clinicians, it may allow for hedging of bets, as in "I think this individual responded to my efforts over the past several months or years but I'm not sure so I'd better point out that he is a psychopath after all, and we all know that they respond poorly to treatment." It may also be the case, especially when a simple assessment with no treatment is conducted, that use of the term is a way, via the self-fulfilling nature of the label, that a client called a psychopath and given a very poor prognosis actually demonstrates the anticipated outcome. No doubt such reasons for employing these labels are less than conscious.

Of course, a simple explanation for using such labels is that it reflects the reality that some individuals are simply "born bad" and remain bad until the day they die, and the label simply reflects this innate badness. This is certainly what theorists like Eysenck (1964) concerned with criminal conduct across the life-span with a heavy biological emphasis would have us accept. The evidence, however, appears to suggest that such a simple view of human nature is untenable. Even prominent researchers within the field of psychopathy point out that there is not consistency across the life-span because there is a marked decrease in criminal activity between the ages of 35 to 45, the psychopathic burn-out (Hare, 1970, 1993; Hare, Forth, and Strachan, 1989). Why apply a static designation to an individual who can or perhaps will alter his/her behavior? Once applied, it is very difficult to obliterate the name. Far too many people, professional and public, accept the saw, "Once a psychopath always a psychopath", and this has serious implications in the clinic and the court (Edens, 2006).

Even if clients resist labels like psychopath, there are still the social consequences of being called a psychopath. These consequences remain less than clear, but they appear to be profound judging from the little research that has been done to date. There is more than anecdotal evidence that the diagnosis of psychopathy has a clear impact on triers-of-fact in criminal cases. Some research conducted in Texas (e.g., Edens, Colwell, Desforges, and Fernandez, 2005) has assessed the impact of a psychopathy diagnosis on jurors considering capital punishment. When a defendant convicted of a capital crime is described as an "incurable psychopath", jury members are much more likely to recommend the death penalty (Edens et al., 2005), even when the individual is a juvenile (Edens, Guy, and Fernandez, 2003). Jurors also appear to recommend harsh penalties in "sexually violent predator" cases when the defendant is described as psychopathic (Guy and Edens, 2003, 2006). The research conducted to date, however, is not only limited by being based in Texas, but the methodology has been limited to simulation research. Further research also needs to examine the impact on triers-of-fact in non-capital offences, including offences involving assault.

One rather sad episode involving the effects of psychopathy remains vivid for me. A mother of one of my clients, a teenager who was incarcerated for an inappropriate sexual relationship with a younger sister, contacted me and asked if I saw her son as a psychopath. I explained that her son, a heavy drug user who displayed a very tenuous grip on consensus reality, displayed none of the behaviors typically ascribed to psychopathy. She insisted on me testing him, and she even told me what test to use. She was very disappointed when I held my ground and denied her demand. As I was informed later by a community-based therapist who treated her son on release, the mother had pursued him with the same request and even became very belligerent when he declined to assess for psychopathy. I wondered why a mother would insist that her son, her only son in this case, was a psychopath so I investigated further. It turned out that he had threatened her life with a kitchen knife just prior to his incarceration and, while she did not press charges, she was now afraid for her life. Despite her concern for her son, or perhaps because of it, she wanted him labeled a psychopath by officialdom probably because she expected a much longer sentence on re-offense, or perhaps just closer police protection, with such a label. A psychopathy diagnosis provided her with a means of protecting herself and her family. Similarly, I was approached recently by a student in the throes of a divorce. She asked if I could see her soon-to-be-ex-husband and call him what she knew him to be, a psychopath. When I asked why she was convinced that he was a psychopath, she was none too clear on the personal characteristics that qualified him for a label like psychopathy, although she did emphasize that he was very self-centered and a pathological liar. I did not proceed further except to tell her that, for a number of reasons, I could not provide the assessment that she requested. No doubt she knew that the divorce proceedings would go in her favor if she could secure a diagnosis involving psychopathy for her husband.

One of the social consequences of psychopathy, and to some extent APD, is diminished access to treatment resources. Such psychodiagnoses may well spell no treatment for some individuals. Clinical lore at present tends to suggest that treatment is ineffective for anti-social individuals despite some reviews to the contrary (e. g., Salekin, 2002). Generally, researchers have reported that treatment is ineffective for psychopathy, even making them more likely to re-offend criminally (Rice, Harris, and Cormier, 1992), although more recent reviews tend to be a little less pessimistic, but only a little (see Harris and Rice, 2003). Certainly my training involved a healthy dose of fear of psychopathic clients. One forensic psychiatrist, a family friend who had all but retired from private practice, sat me down one night to fill me in on the perils of working with offenders, the police, and the courts. When I asked about a private civil suit that he had mentioned only briefly, he told me that he was being sued for malpractice by a former client but that it was entirely his own fault because he knew the man was "an extreme psychopath" before entering into therapy with him. The message that he gave me loud and clear was to avoid psychopathic clients like the plague unless I wanted to waste time, energy, and money, likely ending up in court or a public inquiry.

MEDICINE VERSUS MORALITY

Beyond labeling effects, there is one overarching issue concerning psychopathy that has very troubling implications. Blackburn (1988) argued persuasively that, because it failed the homogeneity test (i. e., because there appeared to be no discrete class or group defined), the psychiatric diagnosis of psychopathic personality was nothing more than a label representing a moral judgment and should be dropped from professional use. The role played by morality in devising and applying psychopathy and all related terminology appears significant. Morality also appears relevant when considering the nature of individuals now called psychopaths.

According to Blackburn, psychopathic personality has been a contentious notion from its inception because it imprecisely targets a set of dysfunctional personality traits that are claimed to be involved in anti-social, or asocial, actions. Setting aside temporarily the issue of the reality and utility of personality traits, the results of such a moral judgment are, all too often, rather extreme sanctions on the moral offender. Murphy (1972) argued from a Kantian position that, because psychopaths operate on their on their own impulsive whims without considering the rights of others, psychopaths are "morally dead" (p. 295). As such, they themselves have no more rights than animals and can be treated harshly. He concluded that, under a just law, "When an individual has been diagnosed a psychopath, his 'rights' may be suspended and he may be subjected to involuntary preventive detention and therapy and perhaps even (if his case is hopeless) to painless extermination." (p. 296). Thankfully, Murphy did not recommend that legal jurisdictions adopt his concluding principle because of a number of serious issues that require consideration and redress (e. g., accuracy of diagnosis, possibility of rehabilitation or remission of psychopathy); unfortunately, as some of Edens' research (e. g.,Edens et al., 2005) on psychopathy and capital punishment demonstrates, harshness in sentencing someone called psychopathic already appears to be the case.

It is all too easy to demean and to dehumanize individuals considered psychopathic, something that even professionals can do however unconsciously. As Lynam and Gudonis (2005) wrote as their final conclusion in their review of the development of psychopathy, "this construct {juvenile psychopathy} seems to identify a particularly virulent strain of antisocial individual and is therefore worth continuing to research" (p. 402). When young people are reduced to disease, and virulent disease at that, it is easy to imagine taking extreme steps against them in order to rid the world of the scourge. The response or potential responses to individuals within a community or a society deemed dangerous is far from trivial. Certainly individuals who are committing criminal acts and downright dangerous need to be dealt with firmly, and they are typically. But what if they are merely devious, cunning, manipulative, unpleasant, and dangerous to their competitors in business, politics, or whatever pursuit they engage in? Are these not the success stories that are to be admired, at least if we ignore the means and focus on the ends? What purpose is there to ascribing their success to some predisposition to nasty character traits or offensive tactics?

The question of psychopathy and the morality of individuals called psychopaths, has been addressed by a number of writers and researchers. Smith (1984) viewed psychopathy not as a disease or disorder but as a different moral path, admittedly extreme, favoring individualism, living in the here-and-now, excitement, and a lack of concern for the welfare of others. As he pointed out, such values tend to be on the rise in the developed world and, perhaps sooner rather than later, so-called psychopaths might embrace a majority moral position. Even if they remain a minority, viewing psychopathy as a personal pathology, especially in the absence of empirical evidence, is a rather limited and limiting view.

The issue of the extent of deviancy of so-called psychopaths has been raised by various investigators in recent years. One empirical study conducted by two Australian sociologists (Ray and Ray, 1982) included a community sample of people who had no criminal records but some of whom scored high on the "Psychopathic Deviate" subscale of the Minnesota Multiphasic Personality Inventory. Ray and Ray (1982) found that there was a significant relationship with a measure of Machiavellianism, or an ability to manipulate social actors to one's own advantage, and they suggested that some psychopathic characteristics are very beneficial given the competitive capitalism that is contemporary Western culture. This view was expanded by

McHoskey, Worzel, and Szyarto (1998) who laid out a detailed argument detailing the parallels between common views of psychopathy and Machiavellianism, where the deception of the psychopath is indistinguishable from the practiced Machiavellian. Both appear to have a similar set of social skills (e. g., quick understanding of opposition or targets, persuasive abilities). They, too, found an association between measures of psychopathy and Machiavellianism, and their conclusion was that the only difference depends on a clinical versus a social orientation within psychology.

More recently, Smith (1999) presented an even more provocative thesis based on his earlier work and the work by social psychologists on Machiavellianism. Psychopaths, for Smith, demonstrate extremely rational thinking of a "practical" sort, where they become self-obsessed in order "to further his/her values" (p. 167). They become adept at self-marketing in order to further their personal successes, incidentally using and abusing those around them but through experience finding no concern for the feelings of others. According to Smith (1999), there is no real difference except that psychopathy is despised while Machiavellianism is prized. Smith saw an unfair and discriminatory class difference—individuals with lower socio-economic status (SES), such as working class minorities, tend to be designated psychopathic and individuals with higher SES tend to be Machiavellian. Different social groups have differential access to resources such as jobs not only on the basis of birth but in part on the basis of how they are described. In this way, drug dealing and illegal gun sales are the "occupations" readily available to low SES psychopaths versus corporate executive and political positions are available to ruthless high SES Machiavellians. Smith proposed, quite seriously I believe, implementing treatment programs for psychopaths that would teach them the skills to enter into the world of high finance, corporate progression, and acceptable occupational pursuits. Clearly, however, skills are only part, and likely a small part, of the rise to respectability—the Ivy League credentials and the requisite social connections would be missing generally for those whose backgrounds included early exposure to ghetto life—but the suggestion is a bold one nonetheless.

Along the same line, Levenson (1992) wrote that psychopathy is not disease but a coherent philosophy of life that entailed at its center self-involvement and the trivialization of others. Levenson argued that, following a consideration of both biological and social explanations of psychopathy, the only reasonable explanation of psychopathy was that it involves learning not to experience social anxiety in situations that most people would find very frightening. Some individuals as a result of their particular social experiences learn to overcome social anxiety and become social risk-takers, with a set of rewards for the successful that would encourage further risk-taking and even lower anxiety. Thus, for Levenson, psychopathy is not a disorder but an effect of learning circumstances. 'Institutionalized psychopathy' (Levenson, 1992, p. 66) is a term used by Levenson to designate the distribution of destructive yet successful social acts across a wide range of activities within the context of a corporate culture. Whether business, politics, or the military, there are no doubt corporations that encourage behaviors that injure or kill others in the pursuit of the corporate agenda, and where success within the structure of the corporation demands acceptance of the values that encourage such values as might is right and those beyond the corporation do not matter. Through this psychosocial account of psychopathy, Levenson viewed psychopathy as much more than a life philosophy or form of consciousness—it is a conscious moral stance. He suggested rather ominously that this stance is becoming more acceptable in contemporary Western corporate life in particular and in the developed Western world generally. Data from a massive U. S. National Institute of Mental Health study might lend some support to this view. As Robins and Price (1991) demonstrated, the prevalence of antisocial personality disorder in the United States is increasing, and it is predicted in part by increasing prevalence of conduct disorders. Troublesome kids are growing into troublesome adults and, unless we assume that some odd biogenetic anomaly over the past half century, a change in socialization must be a primary factor in such an increase. Simply coddling children is not likely sufficient to produce conduct disorders and antisocial disorders, but a general trend toward selfishness, lack of concern for others, aggressiveness, etc.—the "psychopathic traits"—might be sufficient.

Although their positions may be somewhat overstated at times, Levenson (1992), Smith (1982, 1999), and others have raised some important points about the current construct of psychopathy especially concerning the issue of morality. Whatever else they may represent, individuals labeled psychopaths do represent that which we fear and dislike. They are selfish to an extreme, cunning and manipulative. In short, they are dangerous, yet they possess some of the very characteristics that we strive for. Their goals, too, such as cheap thrills and easy money, are ones that many of us can relate to if not desire. Although they may not be the reflection in the mirror that frightens, they may be all too familiar as representatives of our own shadows or darker sides. Evidence to support this 'warped morality' possibility comes from two studies by Glenn et al. (2010). They reported finding that individuals high in psychopathy were less likely to base their self-concepts on moral values, at least normatively defined. Glenn et al. (2010) concluded that psychopaths "may display immoral behavior partially because they do not construe their moral identities in moral terms" (p. 497).

This position, unfortunately, produces an easy step into the question of control and personal responsibility for criminal behavior. Glenn, Raine, and Laufer (2011) took that step and argued that psychopaths should not be held criminally responsible because they have innate neurological deficits that do not allow them to understand fully the difference between right and wrong. Even assuming that we could establish conclusively that a disorder called psychopathy or antisocial personality disorder does involve a serious biological deficit, such an argument seems to re-open the can of worms presented by the 1954 Durham Rule, or sometimes referred to as the Bazelon Test, of insanity. This rather loose insanity test only required mental health specialists on the stand in a court proceeding considering the insanity defense to respond yes or no to the question, "Does the defendant have an identifiable mental disorder or defect?" According to the Durham Rule, if a defendant does have an identifiable psychological difficulty, such as antisocial personality disorder, he or she should be found not criminally responsible because the psychological defect could affect his or her ability to determine right from wrong. The Durham Rule did lead to an expansion of insanity guidelines for a brief time. This legal view of insanity, however, became far too broad and a new rule was quickly established (for details, see Grachek, 2006). We do not need to return to such a situation if we accept that morality can vary depending on social groups and even individual differences and, whatever our personal constructions of what is acceptable in terms of personal behavior short of a complete disconnection with consensus reality, we are responsible ultimately for all of our choices. Those called psychopaths should not be treated more harshly in courts than those not seen as psychopaths but neither should they be granted a free pass to conduct their affairs as they see fit.

Another danger that the psychopath represents as 'other' is that it may spell more successful for the other, whether poor or just "trash". Western values once might have meant embracing hard work, frugality, non-pretentious lifestyles, and selflessness but contemporary Western values point more toward laziness, conspicuous consumption, and self-obsession which psychopaths appear to possess in spades. The apparent rise in psychopathy over the past half century and the rise of American global dominance is not likely mere coincidence. The center for psychopathy studies, as well as concerns about psychopaths, is North America. Perhaps because of our fear of the devious, manipulative, self-centered, lazy, and thrill-seeking among us that we produced, however unintentionally, the monster that is the psychopath, a monster which is now on the loose. The psychopath stalking the back alleys, corporate boardroom, or halls of government is a creation that may be difficult if not impossible to stop, although the avenue of pathology seems to be the wrong way to proceed. Medical or quasi-medical explanations of what can readily be construed as a lifestyle choice based on a particular set of values, however unconsciously accepted, can only convince those who we might want to change their ways that such change is impossible. "My biology made me do it" is perhaps a more compelling reason for not considering possible personal wrongdoing than blaming devils, mothers, or educational systems. If we truly want to address the problem of what some may now define as psychopathy, perhaps we should stop rewarding in a broader social fashion the very characteristics or the values espoused, represented, and/or selected by individuals now viewed as psychopathic or antisocial.

Summary, Conclusion and Recommendations

Psychopathy was and remains a "clinical wastebasket" (Karpman, 1947, p. 364). It represents a category where individuals—whether prisoners, patients, clients, or coworkers—can be placed if they are troublesome, aggressive, uncaring, difficult to deal with, or just plain 'assholes'. There seems to be little professional agreement, still, as to who really fits into the category, and this disagreement might help to explain the continued wooliness of the term, to say nothing of the proliferation of psychopathy variants. Something needs to be done to remedy the situation, and band-aid approaches may not work.

Like any psychological predicate or psychiatric diagnosis, we can and perhaps should ask the question of psychopathy, "Is this a meaningful label?" Gendreau, Goggin, and Smith (2002) asked a similar question, namely "should one continue using the term psychopath at all?" (p. 414), and they decided that it served no useful purpose. Certainly psychopathy continues to pose problems, and Edens (2006) has provided a helpful critique of the current, unresolved problems that can or might hamper forensic clinicians who must face the issues presented by psychopathy. In the face of these problems, psychopathy could be subdivided further as recommended by Skeen et al. (2003) to invent multiple, additional variations of the construct. Such a move might improve treatment success, but it would have little positive impact on the current conceptual confusion and likely little impact on other issues like labeling impact. It would also smack of the Ptolemaeic attempt to make a geocentric view of the universe more palatable. Rather, simply eliminating all related notions, while accepting that there may be similarities among some individuals presenting for treatment which would allow them to be placed in group therapy or a group program together, might be the most parsimonious approach.

Why not consign psychopathy to the wastebasket, period? While this tactic might appear too radical, it may be the best in the long term. Over the past century or two, numerous psychiatric conditions or disorders have been relegated to the garbage bin upon reflection, discussion, and dispute following many concerns and issues with their use. It is rare today to hear about abulia, hysteria, neurasthenia, or nostalgia discussed in terms of psychiatric conditions, but they were popular professional labels in the near past, and some have left their mark on English and other languages through variations on the meanings of the original terms. Is there any reason we need to call people psychopaths? For me personally, this is an easy question to answer. I have tried over nearly 30 years of work as a forensic psychologist to avoid calling anyone a psychopath or anything that hints of such a label. Despite dealing with thousands of individuals variously called psychopaths, APD, sociopathic, or the like, I cannot say that I have ever met someone who I would call a psychopath, although I have met and worked with many individuals who are prepared to sort their social worlds into psychopathic versus non-psychopathic or normal. The benefits of such interpretation for the users might well include a quick and definitive view of people to avoid—the dangerous, the abusive, or the just plain unpleasant—but the costs of viewing people as psychopaths are numerous and serious. We can surely loose sight of another person's humanity rather quickly when disparaging terminology is employed to describe them. Even professionals can objectify and demean individuals deemed psychopathic.

A number of other costs can accrue as well. As mentioned, any individual may accept and internalize the epithet psychopath and may well become such a creature, at least insofar as they understand the characteristics of a psychopath. Other people hearing or reading about the label may come to call and to deal with the 'psychopath' in different and negative ways. They may, for example, deny him or her access to treatment services, punish them by virtue of their label alone (e.g., hand down a more severe custodial sentence in a criminal trial), or simply avoid contact completely.

Having said that I have never met a psychopath is not the same as saying that I have never met someone who is self-absorbed, uncaring of others, impulsive, a thrill-seeker, a habitual liar, and manipulative. I have met many individuals like this, people who might well be labeled as psychopathic, and many have been so labeled, but who are certainly unpleasant to associate with and may be downright dangerous. Not all of these contacts have been in my forensic practice. With respect to professional practice, however, such forensic clients tend to be very difficult to work with but the very ones who should receive valuable treatment resources. They are often high-risk to offend, to inflict serious harm on others, and/or to kill other people. They may well reject offers of assistance especially when young but that does not mean that the offers should not be made. Additionally, their own requests for assistance may not be genuine, or at least not intended for the outcomes that we envisage but for personal gain (e.g., early release if incarcerated, appear to have changed if in family court for a child custody case) but, again, this should not mean that we do not offer, or reoffer, assistance. One implication might be, however, that valuable treatment resources are denied to them after a certain number of failures or feigned attempts. Crying wolf can carry serious consequences.

Forensic mental health professionals need to take labeling effects more seriously. We need to stop calling our clients names in order to avoid possible iatrogenic effects. While some practitioners may doubt that labeling via psychodiagnosis is avoidable, it is possible to avoid labeling clients. First and foremost, we can reject completely certain systems, such as the *DSM*, that employ particularly pernicious constructs, ones that carry moral connotations. Some students when presented with this option react in horror. How could they possibly obtain or retain employment adopting this strategy? My response, only partially facetious, is that there is often a cost to defending personal principles, but I do suggest strongly that the potential benefits more than compensate for any costs. Assessment or treatment reports of non-labelers may be longer than those of labelers, but the clarity purchased at the cost of a longer report should be worth the additional verbiage. If nothing else, the client should be left in a much better position of knowing what issues need to be addressed, and much more likely to have hope that the change necessary can occur.

There are a number of theoretical approaches within psychology and psychiatry that would permit the elimination of psychopathy and like constructs. Personal construct theory (PCT; Kelly, 1955) for me is the most satisfactory option for a number of reasons. First of all, PCT would have all clinicians, forensic and otherwise, avoid all hard-and-fast diagnostic labels. Kelly proposed a novel and useful approach to clinical assessment. He suggested using "transitive diagnosis... {to avoid any} nosological pigeonhole" (Kelly, 1955, p. 775). A transitive diagnosis is a dynamic statement of the important issues at hand in therapy in order to help a client look for "bridges between the client's present and his future" (p. 775). A diagnosis that changes constantly, as the client changes, avoids the trap of being pre-emptive by trying to place an active, struggling client into a box formed by a traditional nosological category, and the box may be more of a Procrustean bed for the individual. Of course, such an approach requires a dynamic theory, such as the one proposed by Kelly (1955, 1963) who viewed all individuals as personal scientists. As Bannister (1979) noted of Kelly's theory, it is one of the few that attempts to set aside the social power of therapists by proposing that clients, like their therapists, are on an equal footing, both functioning like scientists. An egalitarian theory, avoiding distinctions between we-as-psychotherapists and them-as-patients, is perhaps a good starting point to limit the harmful effects of labeling since it would accept that patients or clients have at least as much agency as the professionals who would provide them assistance.

PCT is also helpful in avoiding the problematic notion of personality traits altogether, never mind the really thorny issue of negative or dysfunctional traits that are the bane of the psychopath. Within PCT, the unit of analysis, the personal construct, is a dynamic entity that may allow for stability, so long as one's personal constructs are functional for the individual, as well as change. Some personal constructs can, without a doubt, lead to trouble and a failure to anticipate the future effectively, but such constructs can be purged or altered by any individual, with or without assistance, although the consequences to the system as a whole may be serious. The mid-life change of some so-called psychopaths may be due to the realization that, after years of hitting heads against a wall or bars of a jail cell, something needs to change because what is passing for life is looking pretty grim. Insight, epiphany, 'waking up', or whatever term is more acceptable can apply to those who are nasty just as much as to those of us who are not.

An additional problem that PCT addresses, at least indirectly, is be the morality issue. As I have argued for quite a while (Horley, 1991, 2012), including support from empirical studies (Horley, 1992, 2000), PCT provides a theoretical foundations for values, and morals are simply one particular type or category of values. The variety of psychotherapeutic techniques available to the constructivistic therapist allows engagement, and successes, with a wide variety of clients, including difficult and high-risk ones (see Horley, 2005, 2006, 2008). Through the lens of this innovative theory, we can view anyone, antisocial or not, as having a distinctive set of core constructs that permits him or her to anticipate or to interpret everyday experience. Invalidated personal constructs, especially when the invalidation is extensive and sustained, is an important motivator for individuals to change, sometimes alone and sometimes with assistance. From my experience working with criminal offenders of all descriptions, including many described as psychopathic and personality disordered, everyone can change their construct systems so long as change is the truly desired outcome by the individual for the individual. Change, too, does not necessarily mean individual-level change—we can, if we desire collectively, change the market-driven course that we have set the West on over recent decades down a path that promotes and fosters concern for others, empathy, selfless service to the community or state, and non-aggressive pursuit of dreams and goals. Also, if people can choose change, they can also choose to remain the same and, if this is the choice for individuals called psychopaths, they must be held accountable for their own choices and subsequent actions. In this way, we can avoid the kinds of medico-ethical arguments that might have us absolve so-called psychopaths of criminal responsibility for their acts.

REFERENCES

Bannister, D. (1979). Personal construct theory and politics. In P. Stringer and D.Bannister (Eds.), *Constructs of sociality and individuality* (pp. 21-34). London: Academic Press.

Becker, H. S. (1963). *Outsiders: Studies in the sociology of deviance*. New York: FreePress.

Blackburn, R. (1988). On moral judgements and personality disorders: The myth of psychopathic personality revisited. *British Journal of Psychiatry,* 153, 505-512.

Caplan, P. (1995). *They say you're crazy: How the world's most powerful psychiatrists decide who's normal.* New York: Addison-Wesley Longman.

Edens, J. F. (2006). Unresolved controversies concerning psychopathy: Implications for clinical and forensic decision making. *Professional Psychology: Research and Practice,* 37, 59-65.

Edens, J. F., Colwell, L. H., Desforges, D. M., and Fernandez, K. (2005). The impact of mental health evidence on support for capital punishment: Are defendants labeled psychopathic considered more deserving of death? *Behavioral Sciences and the Law,* 23, 603-625.

Edens, J. F., Guy, L. S., and Fernandez, K. (2003). Psychopathic traits predict attitudes toward a juvenile capital murderer. *Behavioral Sciences and the Law,* 21, 807-828.

Edens, J. F., and Petrila, J. (2003). Legal and ethical issues in the assessment and treat-ment of psychopathy. In C. J. Patrick (Ed.), *Handbook of psychopathy* (pp. 573- 588). New York: Guilford.

Eysenck, H. J. (1964). *Crime and personality*. London: Routledge and Kegan Paul.

Gendreau, P., Goggin, C., and Smith, P. (2002). Is the PCL-R really the "unparallelled" measure of offender risk? A lesson in knowledge accumulation. *Criminal Justice and Behavior*, 29, 397-426.

Glenn, A. L., Koleva, S., Iyer, R., Graham, J., and Ditto, P. H. (2010). Moral identity in psychopathy. *Judgment and Decision Making,* 5, 497-505.

Glenn, A. L., Raine, A., and Laufer, W. S. (2011). Is it wrong to criminalize and punish psychopaths? *Emotion Review,* 3, 302-304.

Grachek, J. E. (2006). The insanity defense in the twenty-first century: How recent United States Supreme Court case law can improve the system. *Indiana Law Journal,* 81, 1479-1501.

Hare, R. D. (1970). *Psychopathy: Theory and research.* New York: Wiley and Sons.

Hare, R. D. (1993). *Without conscience: The disturbing world of the psychopaths amongus.* New York: Guilford.

Hare, R. D., Hart. S. D., and Harpur, T. J. (1991). Psychopathy and the DSM-IV criteria for antisocial personality disorder. *Journal of Abnormal Psychology*, 100, 391-398.

Hare R. D., Forth, A. E., and Strachan, K. (1992). Psychopathy and crime across the life span. In R. D. Peters, R. J. McMahon, and V. L. Quinsey (Eds.), *Aggression and violence throughout the lifespan* (pp. 285-300). Newbury Park: Sage.

Harris, G. T., and Rice, M. E. (2003). Treatment of psychopathy: A review of empirical findings. In C. J. Patrick (Ed.), *Handbook of psychopathy* (pp. 555-572). New York: Guilford.

Honos-Webb L., and Leitner L. M. (2001). How using the DSM causes damage: A client's report. *Journal of Humanistic Psychology, 41*, 36-56.

Horley, J. (2012). Personal construct theory and human values. *Journal of Human Values,* 18, 161-171.

Horley, J. (2011). On the tyranny of professional labelling. *Psychotherapy and Politics International*, 9, 127-133.

Horley, J. (2008). *Sexual offenders: Personal construct theory and deviant sexual behaviour.* New York: Routledge.

Horley, J. (2006). Personal construct psychotherapy: Fixed-role therapy with forensic clients. *Journal of Sexual Aggression,* 12, 53-61.

Horley, J. (2005). Fixed-role therapy with multiple paraphilias. *Clinical Case Studies*, 4,72-80.

Horley, J. (2000). Values and everyday activities. *Journal of Constructivist Psychology,*13, 67-73.

Horley, J. (1992). A longitudinal examination of lifestyles. *Social Indicators Research,* 26, 205-219.

Horley, J. (1991). Values and beliefs as personal constructs. *International Journal of Personal Construct Psychology,* 4, 1-14.

Karpman, B. (1947). Moral agenesis: Toward the delimitation of the problem of psychopathic states. *Psychiatric Quarterly*, 21, 361-398.

Kelly, G. A. (1963). *A theory of personality: The psychology of personal constructs.*New York: Norton.

Kelly, G. A. (1955). *The psychology of personal constructs* (2 vols.). New York: Norton.

Levenson, M. R. (1992). Rethinking psychopathy. *Theory and Psychology*, 2, 51-71.

Lynam, D. R., and Gudonis, L. (2005). The development of psychopathy. *Annual Review of Clinical Psychology*, 1, 381-407.

McHoskey, J. W., Worzel, W., and Szyarto, C. (1998). Machiavellianism and psychopathy. *Journal of Personality and Social Psychology,* 74, 192-210.

Murphy, J. G. (1972). Moral death: A Kantian essay on psychopathy. *Ethics,* 82, 284- 298.

Raskin, J. D. and Epting F. R. (1993). Personal construct theory and the argument against mental illness. *International Journal of Personal Construct Psychology,* 6, 351-369.

Ray, J. J., and Ray, J. A. B. (1982). Some apparent advantages of subclinical psychopathy. *The Journal of Social Psychology*, 117, 135-142.

Rice, M. E., Harris, G. T., and Cormier, C. (1992). An evaluation of a maximum security therapeutic community for psychopaths and other mentally disordered offenders. *Law and Human Behavior*, 16, 399-412.

Robins, L. N. and Price, R. K. (1991). Adult disorders predicted by childhood conduct problems: Results from the NIMH epidemiologic catchment area project. *Psychiatry,* 54, 116-132.

Salekin, R. T. (2002). Psychopathy and therapeutic pessimism: Clinical lore or clinical reality? *Clinical Psychology Review*, 22, 79-112.

Sarbin, T. R. (1967) On the futility of the proposition that some people be labeled "mentally ill". *Journal of Consulting Psychology*, 31, 447-453.

Scheff, T. J. (1964). Social conditions for rationality: How urban and rural courts deal with the mentally ill. *American Behavioral Scientist*, 7, 21-27.

Skeen, J. L., Poythress, N., Edens, J. F., Lilienfeld, S. O., and Cale, E. M. (2003).Psychopathic personality or personalities? Exploring potential variants of psychopathy and their implications for risk assessment. *Aggression and Violent Behavior,* 8, 513-546.

Smith, R. J. (1999). Psychopathic behavior and issues of treatment. *New Ideas in Psychology,* 17, 165-176.

Smith, R. J. (1984). The psychopath as moral agent. *Philosophy and Phenomenological Research,* 45, 177-193.

Szasz, T. S. (1974). *The myth of mental illness: Foundations for a theory of personal conduct* (Revised edition). New York: HarperCollins, 1974.

Verhaeghe, P. (2004). *On being normal and other disorders: A manual for clinical psychodiagnostics.* New York: Other Press.

INDEX

A

B

C

D

E

F

H

I

L

M

P

S

V